With Our Compliments

IMS
The Institute for Management Studies

Over Twenty Years of Excellence in Executive Development

Corporate Headquarters:
505 South Arlington Ave., Ste. 110
Reno, Nevada 89509
702/322-8222

HOW TO GET
FROM NO TO GO

HOW TO GET FROM NO TO GO

The Magic of Negotiating Winning Agreements

ROBERT D. RUTHERFORD, PH.D.

HAYDEN ALEXANDER PRESS
Boulder, Colorado

Dedicated to my children—
Ken, Eric, Douglas, Xenia, and Marla

Published by
HAYDEN ALEXANDER PRESS
1195 Fairfield Drive • Suite 100
Boulder, Colorado 80303
TEL: 303.494.9444 • FAX: 303.494.9408
EMAIL: Roobd@aol.com
www.Rob-Rutherford.com

Copyright © 2000 by Robert D. Rutherford
All rights reserved.

Project editor: *Jody Berman*
Proofreading: *Lori Kranz*
Cover & interior design & production: *Polly Christensen*

"This publication is designed to provide accurate and authoritative information in regard to the subject matter covered. It is sold with the understanding that the publisher is not engaged in rendering legal, accounting, or other professional services. If legal advice or other expert assistance is required, the services of a competent professional person should be sought."

(—from a Declaration of Principles jointly adopted by a committee
of the American Bar Association and a committee of publishers)

Library of Congress Card Number: 98-093070

ISBN 0-9664327-0-3

10 9 8 7 6 5 4 3 2 1

Manufactured in the United States of America

Contents

Acknowledgments — *vii*
Introduction — *ix*

I. Foundations and Negotiating Realities — 1

1. It's just a matter of perspective. — 3
2. Learn to negotiate, then use the skill. — 7
3. The cards we hold in the game of life. — 11
4. Seeing beyond our limitations to the Promised Land. — 15
5. We don't live in an "automatic agreement" world. — 19
6. In negotiating, few things can replace preparation. — 21
7. Where do you go if you don't make the deal? — 24
8. Most things are negotiable, but most things aren't worth negotiating. — 27
9. Learning from your negotiating mistakes. — 31

II. Qualities of Successful Negotiators — 33

10. Empathy versus sympathy—know the difference. — 34
11. Think ahead. — 38
12. Showing up is 80 percent of life. — 42
13. Don't look to others to do for you what you should do for yourself. — 45
14. Never admit defeat. — 48
15. Flexibility—bend or break. — 52

III. Dynamics of the Negotiation Relationship — 57

16. Check in to check out what is happening. — 58
17. Those who implant suggestions govern those who receive them. — 64
18. Ask! Have you ever thought how much you have lost in life by not asking? — 66
19. Agent and third party: no authority to say yes or no but can be your ally. — 69
20. Getting unstuck from a stuck negotiation. — 73
21. Trust is powerful—use it wisely. — 77
22. When you change your mind, let the other party know why. — 81
23. After the deal is signed, it still isn't over. — 86
24. You and others—how people treat you in the negotiation. — 90

IV. Rules and Caveats of Negotiating — 94

25. Don't wobble—know what you want and negotiate to get it. — 95
26. The other party wants to feel good about having negotiated with you. — 100
27. Remember, in negotiating as in life, it isn't over until it's over. — 108
28. Things are not always what they seem. — 110
29. Know the other party's Best Option Outside Negotiation (BOON). — 113
30. Don't make a deal so good that it is bad. — 117
31. You do what you can do. — 119

V. The Give-and-Take to Get to Go — 122

32. "Hollywooding" your concessions. — 123
33. Have a strong rationale for your demands. — 127
34. Never make a negotiating concession without making it conditional. — 133

35. Never accept the first offer—you will never be forgiven 136
36. Guard against splitting the difference. 141
37. Don't concede until you know all the demands that relate to that concession. 143
38. Don't honor an out-of-place or low demand. 146
39. Give concessions that are of high value to the other party and which cost you little. 153

VI. POWER, TRICKS, AND PLOYS 156

40. Beware of a biting dog. 157
41. Escalating authority. 160
42. Good Guy/Bad Guy ploy. 163
43. Power and traps of deadlines. 167
44. Don't let anyone steal your joy. 172
45. Know who the enemy is! 176
46. Power of legitimacy in the written word. 179

About the Author 182

Acknowledgments

Much is owed to a wide spectrum of individuals, both living and deceased. First, let me extend special thanks to the literally hundreds and thousands of individuals I've been privileged to teach, counsel, and consult with over the years in successful negotiator programs in this country and abroad. This book is a definite product of all the wonderful sharing those individuals and organizations have given me.

Second, I am grateful to the authors of the countless books, speeches, seminars, and audio- and videotapes that have had a strong influence on my life and writing. To acknowledge one person would be to overlook so many others. A special acknowledgment to every individual, group, and organization that I have directly negotiated with, resulting in many truly win-win relationships.

A special recognition to my principal editor, Jody Berman, and initial editor, Libby Barstow. Many thanks to the creative design work of Polly Christensen. To those who have read and responded to each of the lessons, your comments were most welcome.

And to my family: my wife, Anneke Rutherford; my sons, Ken, Eric, and Douglas; and my daughters, Xenia and Marla. Only they really know how much this book means to me.

I trust that you will find enjoyment, wisdom, and practical day-to-day applications for both your professional and personal lives.

Best dealings in all that you do in life.

Introduction

Each of the forty-six lessons in *How to Get From No to Go: The Magic of Negotiating Winning Agreements* gives a specific direction to enhance the readers' ability to negotiate the inevitable differences with others and gain what they want from anyone at home, work, or in life.

For many years I have made negotiating presentations throughout the world. Often I would hear, "Rob, why don't you put down these key points just the way you explained them in the presentation, each with an easy-to-remember illustration or story?"

From No to Go represents that effort to bring together proven and vital negotiation concepts and principles contained in an easy, readable lesson.

None of us lives in an automatic-agreement world, and therefore we have to negotiate most of the agreements we have with others—at work, home, and in life. Anything that we cannot exclusively provide for ourselves we must seek from others. This almost always represents some sort of give-and-take negotiation. However, most people do not see themselves as negotiators.

Far too many of life's joys and opportunities are lost for failing to ask for and getting what we want (almost always a negotiated process). There are many given reasons why people fail to learn to negotiate more satisfying and profitable results in their lives, but none of them is valid. No one is negotiating as well as they know how. They therefore incur unnecessary and unrecoverable losses of what might have been.

People of all walks of life would be eager to develop the give-and-take negotiating skills presented in this book if they only realized how easy they are to learn and how much they would enrich their own lives as well as those of others.

—Robert D. Rutherford

SECTION I

FOUNDATIONS & NEGOTIATING REALITIES

1. It's just a matter of perspective.
2. Learn to negotiate, then use the skill.
3. The cards we hold in the game of life.
4. Seeing beyond our limitations to the Promised Land.
5. We don't live in an "automatic agreement" world.
6. In negotiating, few things can replace preparation.
7. Where do you go if you don't make the deal?
8. Most things are negotiable, but most things aren't worth negotiating.
9. Learn from your negotiating mistakes.

1

It's just a matter of perspective

How you view negotiating in general or one negotiation in particular is a matter of perspective. Perspective is the capacity to view things in their true relations or relative importance. Perspective, then, is a viewpoint, position, attitude, or bias. The closer your perspective is to reality, the more in alignment and harmony you are with what is. And from that position of what you are, it is advantageous to view what you want, what is to be in the future.

Your concepts of reality and actual reality are different. The closer they are together, the more accurate you are in assessing what is and what is not.

Many view negotiating as something only for skilled, shrewd, experienced, sharp, smart, crafty, and tough people, and they do not see themselves as being able to learn to negotiate successfully.

How you view the world and particularly how you view negotiating will greatly determine how successful you will be in gaining what you want from others. Do you see the negotiation as too big to take on, too complicated, too difficult, and something that needs to be left to the experts in negotiating?

Or do you see negotiating as a wonderful opportunity to explore ways in which you can get more of what you want and others can get more of what they want from the negotiating parties?

How you see things (your perspective) is all-powerful in negotiating as in life.

DAVID AND GOLIATH

In the biblical story of David and Goliath, the Palestinians and Philistines were at war. When the giant, Goliath, appeared and challenged anyone from the armies of Palestine to do battle against him, all were in fear and fled. Goliath was too big to take on.

Little David was no more than twelve years old. He went to his king and said, "Let me go to battle the giant."

King Saul said, "Son, you are brave, but you cannot possibly battle such an awesome foe. He is too big, too fierce, too strong. Don't you understand that he is too big to do battle against?"

"Not so," said David. "I can defeat him and win victory for Israel."

King Saul said, "Then, go, my son, with the Lord's blessing." David went to battle and slew Goliath.

The children of Israel came to David and asked, "How did you do that? We all believed he was too big to take on."

David said, "Yes, but I believed he was too big to miss." And so it was a matter of perspective. The entire army of Israel saw the giant as too big to take on. One boy saw the giant as too big to miss.
It was a matter of perspective.

Review for just a moment David's perspective in this story. He clearly saw the giant standing in his full armor—an awesome and to some a foreboding sight. He also saw the giant Goliath's strengths and weaknesses. He assessed those weaknesses and determined that Goliath was simply too big for him to miss. It is all a matter of perspective.

What are you going to see the next time you come face-to-face with your next important negotiation? Will you take the view that it is too big to take on, or will you see it as too big to miss? It's your option.

Our important negotiations for work and home need our best and most realistic perspective. One that works to find the golden opportunities, the hidden gold veins, the acres of diamonds waiting only to be seen and applied by the wise and successful negotiators that we all can be.

"Men are not worried by things, but by their ideas about things. When we meet with difficulties, become anxious or troubled, let us not blame others, but rather ourselves, that is: our ideas about things," said Epictetus.

It is not the actual negotiations that we fear as much as it is the idea we have about the negotiations. We worry if we will be listened to. We are preoccupied about giving up too much to the other side. We are concerned about our relative negotiating strengths. We are sure they won't give us what we deserve. It is our ideas about things and not so much the actual things that can get us stressed, worried, and disadvantaged.

> **IT IS NOT THE ACTUAL NEGOTIATION THAT WE OFTEN FEAR AS MUCH AS IT IS THE IDEA WE HAVE ABOUT THE NEGOTIATION.**

*Isn't it strange that princes and kings,
And clowns that caper in sawdust rings,
And common folk like you and me,
Are builders for eternity?*

*To each is given a book of rules,
A block of stone and a bag of tools.
For each must shape 'ere time has flown
A stumbling block or a stepping stone.*
   —Anonymous

WE KNOW HOW TO NEGOTIATE BETTER THAN WE ACTUALLY DO.

2

LEARN TO NEGOTIATE, THEN USE THE SKILL

LEARN TO NEGOTIATE—it is a crucial life skill. No one has ever succeeded well in life and certainly in the business and social world where others walk without being an outstanding negotiator.

No one was born a negotiator, although some children seem to learn the skill at a very early age.

Taking courses in negotiating, reading books on the subject, taking related work in areas such as time management, listening, assertiveness, decision making, and planning all can help—but knowledge and information are of little use unless appropriately applied.

It is such a temptation to settle for so little in our negotiating with self and others. We know how to get more for ourselves and for others than we do. We simply neglect to rightly apply what we know.

We know and unquestionably have experienced times when we didn't apply what we know to dealing with others and lost out—and more than likely the other party lost out as well. I will say to the groups of executives with whom I work in this subject that I am working on an assumption that I want to check out. That assumption is that *no one here today is negotiating and relating to others as well as they know how.*

Now there is often a silence, or someone will indicate his or her objection to such a statement. Then I will say,

TO SUCCEED IN LIFE, YOU NEED TO BE A GOOD NEGOTIATOR.

"Well, if that is not true, certainly the opposite is not true; that is, there is no one here today who is negotiating better than they know how!" Right?

Eagle Flight Training Center

A flock of turkeys was complaining they couldn't fly and soar like the great eagles in the sky, so they enrolled in the eagle flight training school in another part of the land. They made the arduous five-day trip to flight training by foot.

For the next seven days they trained intensively. They acquired great skills, experience, and success in flying. They all soloed and were awarded their eagle flight wings—a proud moment.

Emotions were high. The turkeys thanked their eagle instructors for instructing them in the fine art of flying. They extolled the virtues of the training. They talked about how important the flying skills were that they had just learned. They discussed how they were going to immediately apply these skills in their work and lives.

Then the time came for the turkeys to leave the training center. They gathered up their gear and put it on their backs and then walked the long, arduous road back home—the same road by which they had painfully walked to get to the eagle flight training center.

We neglect to prepare as well as we know how, we fail to listen as well as we know how, we get angry and lose control when we know how to stay in control, we are diverted and lack focus when we could focus, and on the list goes.

The point is that you and I already know how to negotiate better than we are doing. I don't know what that says to you. To me it says, Rob, you had better pay some real attention to what you are doing in the negotiating process, or you more than likely will lose out as well as others, sadly, needlessly.

Often, when making this presentation, I will put a slide on the screen of an eagle soaring; the slide states, "Either soar with the Eagles or walk with the Turkeys." Then, having told this story of the turkeys and the Eagle Flight Training Center, I will ask the group, "Why did the turkeys walk home?"

Not having asked the turkeys, we don't know for sure, but some of the following are unquestionably close:

➤ They didn't see the worth of what they had learned.
➤ They were afraid that other turkeys, seeing them fly, would think they were uppity.
➤ Turkeys don't fly. Even when they know how to fly, they don't fly—that would be against their basic nature and be out of character.
➤ They couldn't break the old habit.
➤ They didn't believe they could really fly.
➤ They were afraid to fly.
➤ Flying was out of their comfort zone.
➤ They enjoyed walking, instead of flying, in some perverted, strange way.

EITHER SOAR WITH THE EAGLES OR WALK WITH THE TURKEYS.

THE CARDS YOU HOLD IN THE GAME OF LIFE (AND ALL ITS INEVITABLE NEGOTIATIONS) MEAN VERY LITTLE—IT'S THE WAY YOU PLAY THEM THAT COUNTS.

- ➤ They would do it sometime in the future, when the timing was better for flying.
- ➤ They wanted to study flying more fully to better understand how and why to fly.
- ➤ They would hire a consultant later, to help them determine the value of flying.

Why the turkeys walked painfully home instead of flying home we may never know, but it is not really important, is it? Why you and I don't negotiate as well as we know how is what is important. None of us want to be like the turkeys in this illustration and not do what we could and should be doing better in the many and continual daily negotiations of our lives.

Our doubts are traitors, and make us lose the good we oft might win by fearing to attempt.
—William Shakespeare

3

THE CARDS WE HOLD IN THE GAME OF LIFE

AMONG THE MOST OFT-ASKED questions relating to negotiation are: "How do I get negotiating power?" "How do I get the competitive advantage?" "How can I successfully negotiate with others who are more powerful than I am?"

Certainly there are times when the other party has the negotiating advantage. At times like this, it seems you need them much more than they need you. Time is on their side. They may have a better Best Option Outside Negotiation (BOON) than you. They may have more resources, more skills, and more strategic alliances to call upon. Perhaps they have even taken an intensive negotiation training course.

Don't be overly concerned. One of the most common mistakes made in negotiation is to attribute too much power to the other party and to minimize our own strengths and power.

> *The cards you hold in the game of life (and all its inevitable negotiations) mean very little—it's the way you play them that counts.*

I love this saying and the meaning it has imparted to all my negotiations and transactions with others. Think about it for a minute. What is the truth of this statement for you?

In negotiating, you and I have more power to get what we want than we think we have. We just need to

AVOID ATTRIBUTING TOO MUCH POWER TO THE OTHER PARTY.

MUCH OF SUCCESSFUL NEGOTIATING IS BASED ON YOUR PERCEPTION OF POWER.

play our cards more wisely. How? you might ask. Take planning as a start—knowing what we want, developing a strategy for getting it. Doing our surveillance work before the negotiation begins. Putting on our Double Vision glasses, so to speak, and seeing the negotiation from the other side as well as ours.

Power is largely a mental state, a state of mind and spirit. But that's not to say it isn't real. Though it may sound trite, there is much truth in the statement

If you think you have power in the negotiating arena, you do; if you think you don't have power, you don't in terms of applying any such power.

What might we be talking about here?

Generally, other people accept the judgments we have about ourselves. For example, it you think you are dumb, people will concur. If you believe that you are worthy of all the good and wonderful things that can come from negotiating and demonstrate such a belief, others will accept that. That is power at your disposal. If you believe that you are a fair and principled person and demonstrate that, others will be prone to accept that as such.

However, if you feel unable to stand up for what you believe in and what is right for you and convey that, others will support that negative perception you have of yourself.

So, then, *much of successful negotiating is based on your perception of power.*

The power you bring to the negotiating process, the way you play the cards in your hand is, for the most part, largely in your mind. The other party may have more information than you have, a stronger position, better timing, a more favorable market position than you will ever obtain, all of which translates into: they are more powerful than you are.

This does not mean that you must either lose or give up so much that it nearly breaks you to get an agreement. What it does mean, though, is that you have to play your cards very wisely and that this is what all these lessons are about: assisting and supporting you to become the best that you can and should be.

Just because your negotiating counterpart has a better hand does not necessarily mean that they know how or will play that hand to their maximum advantage. Opportune moments come and go all the time without being seized. We've all known people who, on the surface, would seem that they should be able to get what they want but don't—people who have graduated from the top universities, come from the finest families, have great talent and intelligence, but have wasted their talents and their advantages.

Recall the story from *Aesop's Fables,* "The Tortoise and the Hare." It is a foregone conclusion that the slowest of rabbits can outrun the fastest of turtles. In this fable the author would have us believe that while the Hare was clearly faster, more talented, and built and born to run, he lost out to the slower turtle because the rabbit—to use the metaphor of card playing—didn't play his cards well. The Hare did not do what he could have done and should have done and would have done if he truly was out to win that race. He miscalculated what it would take to win. He underestimated his opponent—the opposite party—and overestimated himself.

Maybe Yogi Berra was thinking of the Hare when he said, "It isn't over till it's over." The Hare didn't perform even to a minimum level of hare performance. You might say he dogged (or maybe rabbited?) it.

There are many negotiators like the Hare in this Aesop fable, if you like, dogging it. They come into a negotiation, winging it when they could have been expertly prepared. They don't listen, they lack focus, they take things for

CAN YOU IMAGINE PLAYING POKER UNTIL 2 A.M. AND NEVER ONCE LOOKING AT YOUR CARDS?

ARRANGE WHATEVER CARDS YOU HAVE IN WAYS THAT HELP YOU GET WHAT YOU WANT.

granted, they don't check out their assumptions, they misread their opponents, they fail to do their homework, they lose. Although just a fable, "The Tortoise and the Hare" shows us that just because you may be faster, smarter, built better, and have performed expertly in the past doesn't necessarily translate into how you will apply these strengths when called upon to perform in the future.

Arrange whatever cards you have in ways that work to your advantage. Know that if you did all the things you are capable of, you would literally astound yourself and others, too.

Keep in mind, when you think of the following saying, how you play your cards: "No one is negotiating as well as they know how." Certainly, the opposite is *not* true—that is, no one is negotiating better than they know how. So what the other person knows but doesn't do and what you know and will do evens the unleveled negotiation playing fields in the world we live in.

Can you imagine playing poker until 2 A.M. and never once looking at your cards? Truly looking at them and acknowledging what you have and what you can do with them? In negotiating, there are some people who seemingly don't look at the cards they are holding. They do not play them well.

> *The cards you hold in the game of life (and all its inevitable negotiations) mean very little—it's the way you play them that counts.*

May you all play them well for the benefit of all concerned!

Know when to hold them, know when to fold them.
—Anonymous

4

SEEING BEYOND OUR LIMITATIONS TO THE PROMISED LAND

FLYING BACK from John F. Kennedy airport to Denver International, one of my associates sat next to a young woman who caught his interest. As they talked, he couldn't help noticing that she was wearing what he assumed was a wedding ring. But it was on the wrong hand. "I hope I am not being too personal," he said, "but isn't that your wedding ring?" pointing to the ring on her right hand. "Yes, it is," she said. "Well, it is on the wrong hand, isn't it?" my friend said. "Yes, it is," she said, "but I married the wrong man!"

What struck me when I heard this story was not how many, like this young woman, are married to the wrong man, as that is not our subject, but how many are certainly married to the wrong idea about what negotiating is and is not.

"Negotiating is only for experts"; "It really is just another name for hassling, dickering, and haggling, isn't it?"; "It is only for the tough and the shrewd"; "I don't know how to negotiate." Even worse is "I am not a negotiator; I really don't negotiate anything." "They are so much better, stronger, smarter, quicker, more experienced than I am. I don't have a chance of negotiating a good deal with them." On it goes. Any one of these misconceptions could severely limit any of us from getting what we want in negotiating with others. Combine two or three, and you can see the real challenge we have to

ARE YOU MARRIED TO THE WRONG IDEA ABOUT WHAT NEGOTIATING IS AND IS NOT?

THERE IS NO "AUTOMATIC AGREEMENT" WORLD.

breaking through the barriers we have set in our view of negotiating. These are the barriers that limit our ability to get what we want in the "Promised Land" with others at work and in our personal lives.

We were born to negotiate all through our lives, most likely right to the very end of life. The reason why is simple. There is no automatic agreement world. We do, though, live in an agreement world—a world crammed full of agreements implied or explicit. Agreements with our family, friends, customers, boss, government, society as a whole. We seek out agreements in our personal lives, with our livelihood, with our parents, children, and loved ones. It is virtually impossible to have a relationship of any importance and of any length without having it be a negotiated one. When do I talk, when do you talk? What is important, what should be a first priority, and what should be left to a later time? How are we going to spend our time together; what are we going to do together?

"Oh, I don't negotiate," a person might say. My response would be, "Oh, then you have no friends, family, job, living arrangements, contracts, purchases, money to spend or save, or time for things."

One of the missions of this book is to support you in getting past No to Go to make win-win agreements and relationships. The lessons in this book are designed to give you more understanding, knowledge, and skill in the art of giving to others to get from them more of what you want. To live well, to achieve, to have peace of mind and control over your life, you must be an effective negotiator. There is no choice. That is the way it is.

We constantly negotiate and renegotiate the elements of our relationships of all kinds. What we get in life depends more often than not on how good a negotiator we are with those with whom we live and work.

The path to the Promised Land is a give-and-take path that has to be taken with others. The Promised

Land is more a state of being than a geographic location. It is what you want out of life and how you go about getting what you want from yourself and from others. Put another way, it is what you are willing to give to get.

The barriers to the Promised Land are many—the greatest for each of us is ourselves.

"The greatest human temptation is to settle for too little," the Trappist monk, Thomas Merton, reminds us. What was that? "The greatest human temptation is to settle for too little." Why, that could well fill tomes. Perhaps it is our sense of lack of self-worth, cultural conditioning, fear of failure or success, unwillingness to break out of our "comfort zone," unawareness of our real abilities, talents, and possibilities … and you can add to the list from your own personal experience of what is true for you.

Listen to what Nelson Mandela had to say in his inaugural speech in 1994 in South Africa:

> *Our deepest fear is not that we are inadequate.*
> *Our deepest fear is that we are powerful beyond measure.*
> *It is our light, not our darkness that most frightens us.*
> *We ask ourselves, who am I to be brilliant, gorgeous, talented and fabulous?*
> *Actually, who are you not to be?*
> *You are a child of God.*
> *Your playing small doesn't serve the world.*
> *There is nothing enlightened about shrinking.*
> *So that other people won't feel insecure around you.*
> *We were born to make manifest the glory of God within us.*
> *It is not just in some of us; it's in everyone.*
> *And, as we let our own light shine, we unconsciously give other people permission to do the same.*
> *As we are liberated from our own fear.*
> *Our presence automatically liberates others.*

NEGOTIATING IS A GIVE-AND-TAKE PATH TO GETTING WHAT YOU WANT FROM OTHERS.

THE GREATEST BARRIER TO GETTING WHAT YOU WANT IS YOU.

Is it possible that our deepest fear is that we are powerful beyond measure? All of the great teachers from time immemorial have told us basically the same thing: to search within yourself, discover your real inner, higher self, and know that God is within each of us.

Each of us is left to discover the truths about ourselves. Is it true that each of us has a power so potent, so enormous, so great, so awesome, so personal that we deny it and even fear it?

The power you and I have to be extraordinary negotiators of life is awesome. To see beyond your personal set limitation to the Promised Land is within the grasp of each of us.

What each of us does about it is very personal and our choice. This book is dedicated to assisting you in making the right choice for you and all those with whom you come into contact on your way to the Promised Land. Good journeying.

We all know the power to choose how we view the world and that is the most important choice we are continuing making in our lives each and every day.
—**Anonymous**

5

WE DON'T LIVE IN AN "AUTOMATIC AGREEMENT" WORLD

WHY DO YOU WANT to improve your negotiation skills?" That question is asked in almost every negotiation seminar and presentation. In an on-site workshop with one of our corporate clients, a participant raised her hand. She simply said, "I want to continually improve my negotiating skills because I do not live and work in an automatic agreement world." She then gave as an example all of the differences of opinion, perspectives, and needs and wants she had to deal with in and out of her organization. She had to negotiate and renegotiate agreements with clients, vendors, and government representatives. She said she continually was in a give-and-take situation with her associates, her boss, and nearly everyone else she came into contact with at work and at home.

She said, "The better I do at giving and taking, the more I accomplish and achieve in both my work and life. Negotiating for me, then, is truly a life skill that far exceeds just being some kind of special event across some bargaining table over some kind of company contract."

At times I wish there were such a thing as an automatic agreement world. But then, when I reflect on what that kind of a world would look like, I think, "No thank you; I will take my chances and increase my ability to

CONSIDER ANY RELATIONSHIP YOU HAVE OF IMPORTANCE TO BE A NEGOTIATED RELATIONSHIP.

THE POWER THAT YOU HAVE TO BE AN EXTRAORDINARY NEGOTIATOR IN LIFE IS AWESOME.

give more of what others want from me to get more of what I want from them."

Barring discovering and living in an automatic agreement world, all of us negotiate whether or not we like it or whether we even know it. We are always and will always be called upon to give and to take in all of our human relationships.

Consider any relationship you have that is more than fifteen minutes long and of any importance to be a negotiated relationship. This world works by agreements that are invisible, visible, understood, not understood, implicit, explicit, written, unwritten. All of these are open to negotiation as we all function in a negotiated world.

So check out your assumptions about your agreements. Do you really have any, and are they what you think they are?

Don't let the obvious get in your way.
—Anonymous

6

IN NEGOTIATING, FEW THINGS CAN REPLACE PREPARATION

ONE OF THE MOST PAINFUL moments in life is when we have to admit that we were unprepared and therefore not up to the task and lost out.

A major computer hardware firm was in the preliminary stages of a highly important negotiation with their major provider. Competition in the industry was fierce. Pressures on the bottom line were harsh. I began working with the group to enhance their negotiation skills and strategic thinking, especially as it related to this current negotiation.

"Let me look at and review your written plan, your list of negotiation priorities, and the general way you intend to approach the upcoming negotiation," I asked.

"Rob, we haven't really done much formal planning, but we have a general idea of how we plan to negotiate this transaction. Now that we have been confronted with whether we have adequately planned and are prepared, I would have to say we are not," the group leader responded.

If I understood the situation correctly, they would have gone into an extremely important negotiation more or less by the seat of their pants. They had not developed what their priorities were, what they thought the strengths and weaknesses of the other party were. Little

IT IS PAINFUL TO HAVE TO ADMIT WE WERE UNPREPARED AND THEREFORE LOST OUT.

ALL OF US NEGOTIATE WHETHER OR NOT WE LIKE IT OR WHETHER OR NOT WE EVEN KNOW IT.

or no attention had been given to the other side's BOON (Best Option Outside Negotiation) and their own, nor did they have well-thought-out options and an alternative if they didn't get what they originally were asking for. And it was almost assured that they wouldn't get all they would be asking for.

As strange as this may strike you, for a multimillion-dollar firm to be so ill prepared, it probably is not particularly unusual. It seems that lack of planning on the part of the negotiation teams is the rule rather than the exception. All of us are busy. It takes energy and thought to plan well.

The negotiation team filled out a planning checklist that was given to them, asking such things as what they wanted; what they thought the other party wanted; what their strengths were; what the other party's strengths were; what their needs, wants, and fears were; what options were available; and so on. Good negotiating planning doesn't mean that all the bases are covered. It does mean that serious thought has been given to what each party wants, what the possible deal breakers are, what the walkaway points are. When the surprises come, which they undoubtedly will, you will be able to handle it more readily having prepared for the majority of the negotiation beforehand.

In negotiating as in life, few things replace preparation. Think of the alternative to not preparing for an important negotiation. It's simply not acceptable. Yet one of the major mistakes busy people make in and out of business is to shorten preparation time. Going into important negotiations by "winging it" frankly doesn't fly.

Excuses for not planning properly are nearly endless, running from "don't have time," "can't plan for the future," "will plan later when I have time," to "I have to wait for more data," "planning restricts my creativity," and so on, ad nauseum. I suspect we all have our favorite excuses for not doing what we know we should do and what we can and would do if we were to be more effective as negotiators.

In the serious, really important negotiations in business and personal life, failure to prepare is almost a guarantee of losing out to the other party when they have done their homework and are prepared. Some prepare more for a two-week vacation than for a critical negotiation. Dumb? What do you think?

If you don't prepare to win, you'd best prepare to lose out: to lose out on what might have been; the good that could have come from knowing better what you wanted; the other party's needs, strengths, and wants; and the way to get what you want.

Preparation is not limited to getting appropriate and pertinent facts on the negotiated issues, learning about the other party, gathering data and information, and translating all that into powerful negotiating points. It is as much, if not more, about preparing the mind, the spirit, and the body to take on the responsibility of doing due diligence and performing at optimum levels so as to provide fiduciary responsibility to your clients, customers, organization, or whoever it is on whose behalf you are negotiating.

TOO OFTEN, LACK OF PLANNING IS THE RULE RATHER THAN THE EXCEPTION.

Luck is when preparation meets opportunity.
       —Wise saying

PREPARATION 23

7

Where do you go if you don't make the deal?

ALL OF US have had to say at least one time in our lives, "No deal" with someone, somewhere—right?

How do you know when to say "No deal" and walk? Answer: when your BOON (Best Option Outside Negotiation) is better than the alternatives you have in the present negotiation.

Let's say you have been negotiating over the past several weeks with a developer-builder for a home you want to purchase-build in your community. Although you have been able to reach some agreements and receive some accommodations, they're just not enough. So—you say, "No deal" and go to your BOON, which might be: (1) work with another builder, (2) postpone building until a later time, (3) not build at all, or (4) buy an exciting home. The builder then goes to his or her BOON, which probably would be to find a new buyer.

Sometimes it's advantageous for both parties to realize the need to move on. But move on to where? To your BOON, of course. In a sense, both parties have to meet the competitive norms of each other's options.

Imagine for a moment that you are negotiating for a new or used car. If you don't make a deal with the sales-

YOUR BOON DETERMINES WHERE YOU WALK WHEN YOU SAY, "NO DEAL."

24   FROM NO TO GO

person at the automobile dealership, what is your BOON? Go to the next dealership? Buy from a private party? Keep your current car? The salesperson's BOON is to sell to another person—or find a new job!

You can use your BOON as leverage by directing or indirectly letting the other party know how strong your position is outside of negotiating with them. When done right, it makes the other party realize, in part, what they as Party A need to do to get your agreement.

It is important to know your BOON, as that is where you will go if you don't get a deal with the party you are presently negotiating with. Knowing assists you in setting the limits of what you are willing to give up or how much you are willing to accommodate the other party to reach an agreement.

If you don't know what your BOON is, then how do you know how much to give or take to make the present deal a good and fair one? Then answer is basic: You don't.

What, then, should we do? First and foremost, go out and find out what it is. Do your homework. Although you may say, "Rob, I can't be sure of my BOON," and that may be true, I would then say to you, "Any time and energy you spend working to discover what your BOON is in any important negotiation—that is time and energy invariably well spent."

Real pros can use this option information to gain more concessions from the other party. In win-win parlance, this strategy helps explain and show the other party why they t should not be overly accommodating. No one can expect you to take less in a negotiation or—put another way—to give up more in a negotiating situation than you would be required to from another party—that is, your BOON.

Couldn't one argue that, if the other party knows

NO ONE CAN EXPECT YOU TO TAKE LESS THAN YOUR BOON.

IF THE DEAL DOESN'T GO

IF YOU DON'T PREPARE TO WIN, YOU'D BEST PREPARE TO LOSE.

your BOON, then that is all they are going to be willing to give you?

Yes, that makes sense—and in many instances, one party will want to keep their BOON, in part, secret from the other party. The main reason is, if the other party knows the least you will take, then that is all you will get if the deal goes together.

So guard and use information and understanding of your BOON wisely.

> *It is always your next move.*
> —Napoleon Hill

8

Most things are negotiable, but most things aren't worth negotiating

WE CAN WORK WITH a definition of negotiating as an effort to resolve a difference between two or more parties to reach agreement through the give-and-take process.

What is negotiable? In *You Can Negotiate Everything,* a delightful book by Herb Cohen, he suggests that what is negotiable is anything that is a product or result of a negotiation, and of course that is practically everything.

It wasn't some cosmic power that put the price on an IBM computer. Who it was exactly, we may not know. It might have been the corporate headquarters or the regional vice presidents in their annual price and sales meeting, or the price might have been determined according to how much dust there was on this year's model PCs remaining in the warehouse, taking into consideration competition and the new model coming out in three months.

Most things were not divinely priced or decided on, but were decided upon by some rational or irrational human beings. Therefore, following that line of thought, most things have at least the potential to be negotiated.

To negotiate, the other party has to agree to doing so, or else there will be no negotiation. It does not matter how

MOST THINGS ARE POTENTIALLY NEGOTIABLE BECAUSE THEY ARE A PRODUCT OF A NEGOTIATION.

MOST THINGS ARE NEGOTIABLE   27

Before negotiating something, do a quick cost-benefit analysis to see if it's worth the effort.

good or bad you are; if the other party won't enter into the negotiation, no negotiation will take place. The situation had the possibility of being negotiated but not the actuality of it. Not, again, because of some cosmic power setting the can or can't, but because of the human dynamic.

Then it can be argued that because most things are a product of some type of give-and-take, some kind of human decision, most things have the potential of being negotiated: your hotel room rate, the price you pay for your car insurance, the cab fare into the city, the ticket you purchase for the opera, any item on your telephone bill, what you will pay as a commission to the real estate broker, how much you will pay or not pay at an IRS tax audit, for example.

I stay at a lot of hotels each year, as often my work and presentations are at hotels and resorts. Irrespective of the room rate or the hotel, is that rate potentially negotiable, using the above definition of what is negotiable? Yes, it is, as again God did not determine what the hotel room rate would be.

Now ask the next question: Do I want to attempt to negotiate the room rate? I might want to negotiate because I think the rate is too high; the room next door last night was so noisy I could not get a reasonably good night's sleep; the air traffic was extremely loud; the hotel did not provide a gymnasium; or the room was too hot, too cold, too small, did not provide outlets for my computer; and you can continue the list.

There is little or no doubt in my mind that I could negotiate down the hotel rate. The more leverage I have, the better. Leverage is the ability to maximize more from less—to multiple the power to influence with something from another issue.

Now, the other question is something entirely different from whether or not my room rate is negotiable. Do I want to work to negotiate a rate reduction? In most cases, at least for me, no. Why? Because—and you could fill in your reasons. Some of my reasons for not taking the time and energy to negotiate the rate down are simply that. Not that I think the hotel is justified in charging so much for a room that doesn't even have a view or a miniature refrigerator that I can keep my M & M candy, chocolate peanuts, and bottled water in. I don't negotiate because the time and effort it would take are simply not worth it.

But let's say we choose to negotiate the room rate, maybe just to see if it can be done in any particular time. We go downstairs to the front desk. We tell our story to the desk clerk, a pleasant enough person. She courteously tells us she has no authority to handle our demands or request, but that Marilyn Baker, the assistant manager, handles such issues, and she will be at the hotel in five hours at 3:00 P.M.

We meet with Marilyn Baker at 3:00 P.M., and she attentively listens and acknowledges our request. We think, "Aha, finally we will get our demands met." Then she says to us, "If it were up to me, I would grant your request right now, but you know how the hotel business is. I will have to take your problem to the hotel committee on room rate reductions. That committee meets each and every Tuesday evening except the last two weeks of December. I assure you that I will do my very best to get your problem resolved to your satisfaction. Can you call me back Friday, as I am sure I will have an answer for you then." We say "Fine" and leave. On Friday we call three different times to get hold of Marilyn, but she is not available or is out on break or didn't come in today due to an illness in the family. No, there is no else who can help us, so please call back tomorrow. I am sure she will be in and will be very glad to be of help to you.

It is easy to see where this is all leading. It illustrates that although you might be able to negotiate an item to your advantage—like getting the room rate reduced—

MOST THINGS ARE POTENTIALLY NEGOTIABLE BECAUSE THEY ARE A PRODUCT OF NEGOTIATION.

MOST THINGS ARE NEGOTIABLE 29

doing so is simply not worth the time and effort. The cost is simply too high relative to the benefit, imagined or real, that would come from it.

Before thinking of negotiating something, do a quick cost-benefit analysis as to the time and effort, along with the ascertained probability of its being negotiated to your satisfaction. In most cases you find it is not worth the investment.

Now of course there are times when it is, and with the right Successful Negotiator mind-set you go to and enter into the negotiation.

> *To everything there is a season, and a time to every purpose under the heaven.*
> —Ecclesiastes 3:1

9

Learning from your negotiating mistakes

The dictionary defines *mistake* as "wrong action or statement proceeding from faulty judgment, inadequate knowledge, or inattention."

To make mistakes is human. It is better to learn from other people's mistakes—simply for no other reason than we can't live long enough to make all the mistakes that are possible in a single lifetime.

No matter what level of negotiating effectiveness we operate from, we are bound to make mistakes of judgment, omission, or commission; perhaps we misread someone's intentions, did not listen adequately, and so on.

To minimize the negative penalties and repercussions of mistakes made, ask yourself, "What am I to learn from this experience?" When you give up a concession without making it conditional in negotiating, what lessons are you to learn from this?

Say you worked on the faulty assumption that the other party would not have been willing to accommodate your interim financing—but in actuality they would have. What lesson is there to be learned here?

I wrote a book titled *The Twenty-Five Most Common Mistakes Made in Negotiating ... and What You Can Do About Them.* Listed were such mistakes as "Failing to negotiate when I could have, should have, and would

When you make a mistake, ask yourself, "What am I to learn from this experience?"

MOST OF US WOULD BE SURPRISED HOW EASY IT IS TO CORRECT A NEGOTIATING MISTAKE.

have if I had been more effective;" "I attributed too much power to the other party"; "I failed to manage the other person's expectations"; "I defined winning as beating the other party."

Take the first mistake, "I failed to negotiate when I could have, should have, and would have." What does that say? Does it say, "I do not feel I am worthy of all the good things that can come from negotiating?" or "I fail to see the opportunities to gain more of what I want and give others more of what they want from me?" "I believe that you don't have the skill and mind-set to negotiate successfully?"

Every mistake listed in that book can be corrected. Most of us would be surprised at how easy it is to correct the mistakes we make in negotiating—taking little talent, time, or effort. But we don't. It is easy to correct them, true; but it is also true that it is easy not to correct them. Ironic, isn't it? It is easy to say "Thank you" to someone for the courtesy they extend us, but it is also easy not to say "Thank you." It is easy to floss our teeth, but it is also easy—what? Not to floss our teeth. That is a problem. Many good things that are easy to do are also easy not to do.

And so it is with making mistakes in negotiating.

We should be careful to get out of an experience only the wisdom that is in it—and stop there; lest we be like the cat that sits down on the hot stove lid. She will never sit down on a hot stove lid again and that is well: But also she will never sit down on a cold one anymore.

—Mark Twain

Section II

Qualities of Successful Negotiators

10. Empathy versus sympathy—know the difference.
11. Think ahead.
12. Showing up is 80 percent of life.
13. Don't look to others to do for you what you should do for yourself.
14. Never admit defeat.
15. Flexibility—bend or break.

10

Empathy versus sympathy—know the difference

THE BIBLICAL PRINCIPLE of seeking first to understand the other person and then being understood by that person in return is as important today as at any time. Relating this principle to negotiating, we can say that negotiating is an effort to meet the needs of the parties by reaching an agreement by the give-and-take process.

It is much easier to meet the needs of the other party (as well as our own) if we first know what those needs are. In both negotiating and selling, seldom is the wise thing to enter into a sale-negotiation situation trying to convince the other party of something before knowing what their needs and concerns are.

Before you begin any negotiation, put yourself in the other person's position. Work to understand how they feel about the situation, what they might fear, need, want. By being empathetic you allow yourself to identify with and truly understand the other person's perspective.

What I am referring to here is being empathetic, which sometimes is confused with being sympathetic. Instead of giving a dictionary definition to differentiate the terms, let me give an example of the differences.

Imagine you are on an oceangoing vessel. On the top deck you see someone leaning over the railing getting seasick. Now, if you were into sympathy, you might go

> **IT IS EASIER TO MEET THE NEEDS OF THE OTHER PARTY WHEN WE KNOW WHAT THEY ARE.**

up to the person and say, "Oh, I am so sorry you are seasick. Is there anything I can get you? Perhaps some hot tea or warm broth?"

That would be a nice, loving, caring thing for you to do. You feel bad about their situation. You are showing sympathy here.

Let's say you are again on the top deck and see this same person leaning over the railing having seasickness. Now if you were into empathy, you would probably go over and stand next to that person, lean over the railing, start to feel sick, or actually become seasick yourself.

Why? Because you had so successfully put yourself in that person's position that you literally took on their experience and became seasick.

Although this is certainly an extremely dramatic example of empathy as contrasted to sympathy, it does illustrate the point of putting oneself in the position of another in order to see the world from their viewpoint, to attempt to feel how they might feel, to be as much at one with them as possible.

Using empathy is a powerful negotiating skill and strategy. In part it is accomplished by watching and listening carefully and by being committed to truly understanding the other party in the negotiation.

I had just finished a presentation to a group of law enforcement officers at the FBI academy at Quantico, Virginia. I had used this story of seasickness to illustrate the difference between sympathy and empathy. One of the officers came up and remarked about the story. He said, "You know, more often than not, the best homicide detectives in our division have almost always been the most empathetic to the killer." Not sympathetic, I hope, but empathetic. Those particular homicide detectives had been able to put themseves in the position of the killers; they could think and feel what the killer might be thinking and feeling; they could anticipate what the killer might do.

BEING EMPATHETIC DOES NOT NECESSARILY MEAN YOU AGREE WITH THE OTHER PERSON.

Being empathetic with your counterpart and acknowledging their position does not necessarily mean that you agree with them. In fact, you may often disagree. But in empathizing with another, you are able to state that you understand them, regardless of your own feelings about the situation.

During the Los Angeles riots of the 1990s, Bobby Green was one of those individuals who came to the aid of Reginald Denny who was being beaten by the unruly street mob. When he was asked why he risked his life to stop the beating of a person he had never seen or known, Bobby Green said, "It felt like I was getting hurt."

Bobby Green had put himself, figuratively and then literally, in Reginald Denny's position. He empathized with him.

Demonstrating empathy is not unlike the skill shown by novelists, actors, and psychotherapists who know their subjects so well that they at times take on those subjects' characteristics. They can predict the actions, thoughts, feelings, fears, and idiosyncrasies of the other person. Actors, during the time they are preparing and acting the part of individuals, have been known to nearly literally become the characters they are playing.

Rabbi and author Joseph Telushkin, writing in his insightful book *Words That Hurt, Words That Heal,* tells a true story about a ten-year-old boy living in Oceanside, California, who had just been diagnosed as having cancer. Telushkin writes, "The doctors prescribed ten weeks of chemotherapy, during which, they warned him, all his hair would fall out. To avoid the anxiety and pain of watching his hair gradually disappear, the youngster had his entire head shaved."

Telushkin goes on to write, "One can only imagine Ian's feelings a few days later when he returned to school, prematurely bald, and found that the thirteen other boys in his fifth-grade class, and their teacher as well, greeted him with their heads completely shaved." This represents not only empathy but sympathy as well and demonstrates that understanding and caring in action.

> *Whatever you may be sure of, be sure of this—that you are dreadfully like other people.*
> —James Russell Lowell

11

THINK AHEAD

NEGOTIATION is much like chess. If you don't think ahead, you are going to get jumped and ultimately checkmated.

While at the beach in Santa Monica, California, on a Saturday morning, I found myself watching and being intrigued by a group of sidewalk chess players. The way these old-timers played—intense, focused, committed to the playing of the game—one might think they were playing for the world chess title.

Sitting on the table next to the players was a timer setting the time parameters in which they had to make their moves. It probably wasn't any more than thirty seconds. Certainly there was no time to develop elaborate chess stratagems or to reflect on the dynamics of human behavior relative to the art of chess playing.

Nor, if they were to have a chance to win the game, could they be clueless as to what might be the options of the other player, B, to any move they might make in playing Player B.

As they made their quick moves, I got the distinct feeling that each of the players had played this game before, many, many times. Their often instant response to each other's moves seemed like clockwork. They had already anticipated, visualized, and responded in their minds to the other player's move before the move was made. They moved their pawns, their knights, and their other pieces according to a game plan. They protected their king, knowing that to lose their king meant the game would be over.

IN NEGOTIATING, AS IN CHESS, ONE WRONG MOVE EASILY LEADS TO CHECKMATE.

Strategic thinking is critical to winning in chess. One wrong move easily leads to checkmate.

As I left the game area and continued my walk down the boardwalk, it occurred to me that in some ways negotiating can be likened to playing a chess game. The successful negotiator has a well-thought-out game plan, and anticipates the consequences of his actions before he acts, reads, and reacts to the other party.

Much like the chess players, successful negotiators recognize the key pieces in their negotiation, know what can be given up and what cannot, and strive to position themselves for the real win—gaining what they truly want.

Unlike chess, fortunately, negotiations do not have to be win-lose events. The Successful Negotiator crafts and negotiates in ways that more often than not lead to satisfaction for both parties. In fact, a good argument can be made that if the negotiation isn't good for both parties, a new negotiation should be effected.

In real life, there are countless times when even experienced and professional negotiators don't think ahead, fail to prepare, go into a negotiation winging it (which does not fly), and come up short. All too often, both parties then fail to achieve the most they could have mutually gotten out of the negotiation.

Opportunities for gain are overlooked. Much time is wasted in unnecessary game playing. Trust is forgone, and distrust sets in. Ploys and tricks become the standard rather than the exception.

In more serious and complex negotiations, getting a mutually accepted agreement is hard enough without trying to checkmate the other party. Save that for the chess boards.

Lacking a well-thought-out, solid game plan can lead to being checkmated, assuming that is the intention and goal of the other party. They have jumped you even when you were thinking ahead. You are faced with an unpleasant

> **OFTEN MORE CAN BE ACHIEVED BY ALL PARTIES IF THEY NEGOTIATE MORE EFFECTIVELY.**

TO GET FROM NO TO GO, HAVE A WELL-THOUGHT-OUT STRATEGY IN MIND.

surprise! You think that you are checkmated. Probably not so. What can you do?

➤ Call time-out, remain silent, call for reinforcements, call on your counterpart's sense of fairness, threaten to retaliate, retaliate, give them a chance to correct the error of their ways, ignore it all, go your own way as if nothing had happened.

➤ The other party may be bluffing; they may be testing your resolve. They may genuinely think that what they demanded is rightfully theirs for you to give them. But that does not mean that you should give it to them.

➤ Point out to your counterpart why it is not to their advantage to treat you in an unfair and hardnosed way. (For instance, it will impair any future business dealings; you will work hard to make sure they pay for their wrong acts against you; word gets around about how they negotiate, adversely affecting future negotiations with other parties; their playing hardnosed usurps much of the creative, collaborative working things out together that is so often the critical part of the most successful kinds of win-win negotiations.)

➤ Anticipate the consequences of your moves.

➤ Keep clearly in mind why you are in the negotiation and what you will do if you don't make this transaction.

➤ Accept the reality of the situation; cut your losses and live to return to a better day.

To keep on with our chess illustration, master chess players follow a strategy: They anticipate their counterpart's next move and its consequences and best responses, and so think ahead to win the game. Likewise does the successful negotiator think ahead and anticipate the consequences. The end object of getting from No to Go is not to beat the other party but to gain what you desire from the exchange.

In most negotiations, if conducted rightly, all parties can be winners to the extent at least that they are better off for having gained a negotiated agreement than if they had not reached one.

To continue the reference to chess, if you end up being the party that has checkmated your counterpart, you might want to question if that is really a good thing—for you and for them. Trust, creativity, and working for enhanced relationships to gain even better results will preempt checkmating the other side. But then again, we are not playing chess, are we?

And, unlike chess, giving up something does not mean that you lose—it can be viewed as a golden opportunity for you to get something greater in return.

Epictetus said, "No man is free who is not master of himself." Depend on the rabbit's foot if you must, but remember it didn't work very well for the rabbit, did it?

ANTICIPATE THE CONSEQUENCES OF YOUR MOVES AND THOSE OF THE OTHER PARTY.

> *There is a tide in the affairs of men which, taken at the flood, leads on to fortune.*
> —William Shakespeare

THINK AHEAD

12
SHOWING UP IS 80 PERCENT OF LIFE

I HAVE ALWAYS REGRETTED not purchasing a set of special bookends that I had seen displayed in a little antique shop in Laguna Beach, California. I had been out on the West Coast for a business trip and had a morning free and was browsing.

I saw these two objects that would serve as a perfect set of bookends for my office. I had never seen anything quite like them. Different, to be sure. I looked at the price in the window and it struck me as on the high side (I am not sure how I came to that conclusion, as these items were so unusual; value had to be in the eye of the beholder).

Anyway, walking into the little shop, I picked them up, admired them, thought how I could use them on my bookshelf, and looked at the price, thinking they were still priced a little high. Putting them back down in the window, I walked out of the store never to return, and ever since have regretted not buying those bookends!

Even if I had paid the price asked for, they would have been wonderful. So why didn't I? Really I don't know. I've often thought about it: Perhaps I just didn't want to make the effort to negotiate that day. Was I afraid that I would get into some kind of argument? I remember thinking the owner would not move on the price. I can come up with lots of guesses as to why I didn't buy those wonderful bookends.

So here I am, supposedly a pro at negotiating, and I never gave the proprietor of that store a chance to say no, yes, or maybe. I simply did not "show up" to buy, negotiate, or arrange to get these bookends. That was not a very gracious thing I did to the owner of that small shop, that is, not giving him any chance to make a sale and to give me the opportunity of getting a unique pair of bookends.

It is very difficult to negotiate when you are not "there" in any negotiating way. It makes no difference if the negotiation would have been an easy, profitable, and enjoyable one or not. It makes no difference if you would have received extraordinary value, as would the other party. None of this makes any difference. None of this counts when you don't show up.

Taking this out of the negotiating process for a moment, how much is lost by parents not showing up for their children's important events: baseball game, school play, teacher-parent conferences? Or not showing up at the voting polls, at the church of your religious preference? Or showing up physically but not really being there mentally?

When I wrote *The Twenty-Five Most Common Mistakes Made in Negotiating... and What You Can Do About Them*, the first mistake listed was "I failed to negotiate when I could have, should have, and would have—if I had been more effective."

What strikes me as so sad is how many times most all of us have failed to enter into a negotiation with our spouses, family, customers, suppliers—when all parties would have mutually gained from the agreements that would have been reached.

Excuses for not showing up run the full gamut of human inventiveness and ability to lie to ourselves. Would you like to add your favorite to the following masterful excuse list?

➤ I didn't have time.

➤ I didn't really want it anyway.

SHOWING UP AND REALLY BEING THERE IS A POWERFUL ADVANTAGE IN ANY NEGOTIATION.

SHOWING UP IS 80 PERCENT

- ➤ They wouldn't have given me what I asked for in the first place. (How wonderful to have so clear a crystal ball!)
- ➤ I will do it sometime later.
- ➤ The dog ate my negotiating homework notes.
- ➤ Negotiating is for wimps.
- ➤ Negotiating is for ... (add your own: for pros, for the experience, for union-management types, etc.).
- ➤ I will lose more than I will gain.
- ➤ They might take advantage of me.

Showing up and just being there and really being there is a powerful human practice. Try it sometime. "To try and fail is life, but to fail to try is to suffer the inestimable loss of what might have been" can remind us of the importance of showing up. It is hard to get past No to Go if you are not there in the first place. Obvious, isn't it?

> *This time like all times is a very good one if we but know what to do with it.*
> —Ralph Waldo Emerson

13

Don't look to others to do for you what you should do for yourself

SELDOM IS HEARD from successful negotiators: "Why didn't you (do this or that)? You *should* have—it was your responsibility." "I didn't know that. I thought *you* were going to take care of it. You didn't tell me ..."

After one particularly difficult and dark period of my business and personal life, when nothing seemed to be going right, a trusted board member said to me after one of our acrimonious meetings, "Rob, don't look to others to do for you what you should be doing for yourself."

I had been "delegating" responsibilities to certain staff who were either unable or unwilling to follow my wishes. I also looked to my attorney and CPA to do things in an accurate and timely manner, but I should have taken more responsibility for making sure that the things had gotten done right.

In the end, the one person responsible for the company and its actions was not the staff, not the management team, not my attorney, not my CPA, but me. Finally, when government authorities questioned certain

Check out your important assumptions.

When Not to Look to Others

Do what you and only you can do for yourself, which often means negotiating for what you want.

actions that had been taken, everything ultimately came back on my shoulders.

All of the "Well, I depended on my attorney for that," and "I thought the management team understood what they were doing," and "I delegated that to my staff"—didn't absolve my role and responsibility. The buck stopped at my desk, and the penalties of others' mismanagement resided with me as owner of the company.

As in life, so it is in the negotiating process. Certainly others may be responsible for getting you certain necessary information for the upcoming negotiation. You depend on staff for various reports. You count on your team to make good things happen in the negotiation. *But do not look to them to do what you should be doing for yourself.*

For example, make sure the reports are correct before going into the negotiation. Check out your important assumptions. The line between what you should be doing for yourself and allowing others to do for you is not always clear. It's a challenge to get as clear as you can to allow yourself to achieve what you want in your multifaceted negotiations with others.

Take care of the business that no one else cares about or can do as well as you. There are certain things reserved specifically for you and no one else. Perhaps they are your responsibility to begin with, or maybe only you can do them; it could be that you are the only one who really cares or profits from them.

Simply, the dictum is: You are it. You are the only one who, in the last analysis, is responsible for you, your behavior, and the results. As you look to others for help—your attorney, staff, co-workers, family, spouse, children—ask yourself, "Am I looking to others to do things for me that I should be doing for myself?"

Don't look to your negotiating opposite to do your homework for you. Instead, look to the other party to do what they think is the best thing to do for themselves. Don't expect them to take care of you. That is not their job. That is not what they are being paid to do.

Don't look to others to do for you what you should do for yourself. Successful negotiators take care of themselves. They pay attention to important things that they alone are responsible for and do not pass them off on others.

SIMPLY, THE DICTUM IS: YOU ARE IT.

> *To thine own self be true.*
> —William Shakespeare

14

NEVER ADMIT DEFEAT

"Never admit defeat, unless you are absolutely convinced ... and even then keep your mouth shut and wait 'til Monday," writes Michael A. Gilbert in *How to Win an Argument*: "The rule means that you should never hastily concede defeat except in circumstances necessary to your well-being (to keep your job or save your marriage, for example). It is possible to admit defeat later, but at the time of argument it is almost always inappropriate to concede."

Gilbert is not talking directly about negotiating; nevertheless the rule "Never Admit Defeat" must be part of the arsenal of the successful negotiator.

The advantages of applying this rule include:

➤ The chance that new evidence will appear that will support your position and defeat your opposite number.

➤ Even if you do have to concede, your concession (or defeat, if you want to call it such) will have been more fully earned, which will enhance the chances of its being appreciated and valued more by the other party. They will have worked for that concession.

➤ Prudently deferring admission of defeat allows you to do your due diligence and feel more secure about having made the decision to concede on a particular issue.

> How many times in negotiation with the other party have we said something, volunteered information on something only to have it work to our detriment?

Most disagreements and negotiable points are not over facts like whether Washington, D.C., is the capital of the United States or whether Dostoyevsky wrote *The Idiot* or whether most American cars run on gasoline. (Although there are some people who could figure out a way to argue against all three of the above—but do you really need them in your life?)

Most disagreements or negotiations are over issues like values, who is responsible and for what, who should get what from whom, who is right and wrong, the price to be paid for this commodity, what the service should include. These are opinions, points of view, interpretations of reality, but not pure facts.

Disagreements, then, are conflicts or differences between people over the way they see things. We all perceive reality differently. It doesn't mean necessarily that one is right and the other is wrong. Just different.

You might recall the poem about the six blind men of Hindustan who each saw the elephant a different way. All were correct in their limited understanding of what it was they were touching. Because of that, they all drew incorrect and misleading assessments of what it was that they had touched. None of them could touch and therefore appreciate the whole—a thing called an elephant.

Recall also in any negotiation that the negotiators have limited vision. None has all the facts, all the knowledge, all the correct perceptions of the matter at hand. And when they do, these are beliefs and opinions and not solid, indisputable facts.

What happens in so many negotiations is that one party tries to impose their views and wants on the other

MOST DISAGREEMENTS AND DIFFERENCES IN NEGOTIATING ARE NOT OVER FACTS BUT OVER INTERPRETATION OF ISSUES.

NEVER ADMIT DEFEAT 49

party on the assumption that their views, concerns, and demands are the right ones.

Look at your own life and what it is that you and your spouse argue over and attempt at times to negotiate. Opinions, fears, wants, needs, points of view. Not on what your mother's name is, or how many children you have, or what a loaf of bread costs down at the supermarket (although I have known people who somehow find the time, energy, and interest to argue over the above).

How many times have you given in to some demand and later thought of a good reason why you didn't have to? If you have to concede on a point—that is, if you have to admit that you are either wrong or defeated—wait and let the weekend pass.

Michael Gilbert quotes from the German philosopher Arthur Schopenhauer, who wrote in *The Art of Controversy:* "The argument which would have been our salvation did not occur to us at the moment. Hence we make it a rule to attack a counter-argument, even though to all appearances it is true and forcible, in the belief that its truth is only superficial, and that in the course of the dispute another argument will occur to us by which we may upset, or succeed in confirming the truth of our statement."

What made imminently good sense at the time might look very different the next day. Many times in negotiating, we don't think of the right thing to say, the right proposal or counterproposal to make. We are at a loss for a reason to disagree or to say no. The "salvation," as Schopenhauer puts it, is not readily apparent at this moment.

In most cases we don't know how important or how attached the other party is to a position or proposition. By refuting the reasons for their claim, you refute their claim. More than one party has backed down or re-

DISAGREEMENTS ARE BETWEEN PEOPLE WHO HAVE A DIFFERENT VIEW OF WHAT IS AND ISN'T.

treated from the demand when the other party refused to admit defeat and go along with it.

Remember: All conflicts and disagreements are between people who have different viewpoints on what is and isn't. None of us perceive the world the same way. Simply because the other party does not see things the way we do doesn't mean that we have to be threatened by that and that we have to agree with them to be agreeable with them.

Protecting yourself, you have to be aware that the other party is most likely constantly observing you and ready to take advantage when the time appears ripe.

> *Nothing in the world can take the place of persistence. Talent will not; nothing is more common than unsuccessful men with talent. Genius will not; unrewarded genius is almost a proverb. Education will not: The world is full of educated derelicts. Persistence and determination alone are omnipotent. The slogan "press on" has solved and always will solve the problems of the human race.*
> —Calvin Coolidge

15

Flexibility—bend or break

COUNTLESS NEGOTIATIONS have gotten stuck and the parties have reached deadlock because they simply could not bend, they could not adjust, they could or would not see other ways of closing the deal.

Of all the skills that we develop as successful negotiators of the give-and-take of our lives, flexibility ranks as one of the most important, for by definition negotiating is a give-and-take process in which the parties begin at one position and end up at another.

Flexibility is the ability to respond to and change in new situations. It is the awareness that there is no one single absolute answer to the negotiating situation. It is the mindfulness that there is more than one alternative or option open to us.

Isn't it just possible that you may not get everything that you demand in any particular negotiation? You may not get that 20 percent salary increase or receive a price reduction of 10 percent on the line items outlined or get the party to agree to an extension of the loan. Then, when one demand or approach does not work, the successful negotiator selects another one. Many roads can lead from No to Go.

Isn't this vacillation, being indecisive? Aren't you wobbling and not knowing what you want and how to get it?

FLEXIBILITY IS THE GATEWAY TO GETTING FROM NO TO GO.

At first that might seem to be true, but to hold to something from yesterday that is proven wrong today would be counterproductive if you could set it right. And to be held to something today that tomorrow proves untenable would be tantamount to imprisoning yourself.

This is particularly true in negotiation because of the basic nature of its give-and-take process.

Only a foolish negotiator would get stuck in a position when that position is not going to be acceptable to the other party. The from-No-to-Go negotiator keeps clear which issues are the must-haves and which have some give in them. He or she assesses the reality of each given negotiation and, where advantageous, shifts positions, restructures demands, and assesses the costs and benefits to be derived from their new position.

There is a constant search on the part of any successful negotiator to find viable alternatives to getting what he or she wants.

It is not vacillation and mindless pursuit of this and then that. It is a focused, goal-oriented, need-based system that searches out the best that each negotiation has to offer. Flexibility recognizes the world as it is. At times, in order to gain advantage from a negotiation, one has to give up something, be willing to create something, be open to new perspectives and ways of getting the job done—all demanding the ability to bend, the agility to see things not seen by the rigid- mind-set mentality.

The world and all that is in it have never faced such speed of change as today. Skills to manage this change in order not only to survive but to thrive are required. Positive flexibility and adaptability play an increasingly important and vital role in our daily lives.

FLEXIBILITY IS THE ABILITY TO RESPOND TO AND CHANGE IN NEW SITUATIONS.

FLEXIBILITY

Two trees, one an oak and the other a willow, faced the full brunt of the hurricane force. One broke under the relentless winds; the other withstood the force. When it was over, the oak tree lay torn and uprooted, but the willow had withstood the winds.

The oak tree was too rooted in its stand, unable to be flexible and bend with the wind. The willow tree adapted to the storm, bent with the winds, where the oak tree refused to bend, thereby being broken by the winds. The oak tree was stronger but more fragile; it was more deeply invested in its surroundings but not adaptable to the changes brought by the severe and ruthless winds.

We live in a world that is changing, often, it seems, at record-breaking speeds. We stand challenged to either adapt or drop out. The oak tree, although solidly rooted in the ground, could not adapt when challenged by the storm. The wind did not honor the oak's roots; it did not care that the oak had lived a long time and had done fine deeds and was firmly rooted in the earth.

More and more, the quality of adaptability, of being able to judge and gauge the flow of events, is a virtue in our changing world. It is our hardening of the attitudes rather than of the arteries that will be our demise. (Perhaps in some ways, hardening of the arteries is related to hardening of one's life views and attitudes.)

The other party has made a demand on you that you

had not planned for or even expected. It has caught you off guard. You think about it and at first close your mind to its possibilities. It strikes against what you considered you must have. It wouldn't work. Then you begin to open to other possibilities. You begin to see worth in the demand, at least from the other party's point of view. You are able to adjust your thinking and can and do go along with their demands, although you are not particularly excited about them. You do receive, though, a significant obligation from the other party to give you what you will later demand.

At this point you may be challenging me as to the real difference between being flexible and being wobbly. It all has to do with purpose and end results desired and sought after.

I live in the Rocky Mountains. When driving up a mountain, you don't stay in high gear, even if you could. Either your car will automatically make the shift to a lower gear for you, or if you are driving a stick shift, you will do it, that is, if you have a reasonable understanding of how to drive in the mountains.

Apply that analogy to negotiating. Shifting gears, regrouping, assessing alternatives, being aware of your BOON (Best Option Outside Negotiation) and alternatives within the current negotiation, testing, probing, and realigning, are part of the master plan of successful negotiating.

Inflexibility may have its merits in life, but it is not a revered trait for negotiating. If you will not give or adjust, adapt or create alternatives from your original position, that may be the right thing to do. But you certainly are not negotiating. Negotiating is a give-and-take process that by its very nature requires flexibility—and for successful negotiating to take place, the right kind of flexibility is necessary to get the agreements you desire.

> **IT IS THE HARDENING OF OUR ATTITUDES RATHER THAN OF OUR ARTERIES THAT WILL BE OUR DEMISE.**

FKEXIBILITY

> *He who attempts to resist the wave is swept away, but he who bends before it abides.*
> —Leviticus

Section III

Dynamics of the Negotiation Relationship

16. Check in to check out what is happening.
17. Those who implant suggestions govern those who receive them.
18. Ask! Have you ever thought how much you have lost in life by not asking?
19. Agent and third party: no authority to say yes or no but can be your ally.
20. Getting unstuck from a stuck negotiation.
21. Trust is powerful—use it wisely.
22. When you change your mind, let the other party know why.
23. After the deal is signed, it still isn't over.
24. You and others—how people treat you in the negotiation.

16

CHECK IN TO CHECK OUT WHAT IS HAPPENING

THE OFT-QUOTED COMMENT, "When you assume, you make an ass out of you and me," probably is easy for most of us to relate to. We have to make assumptions scores of times daily—assumptions about what is right and wrong, what needs to be done, and what can be left to later for never.

In our important dealings with others, we have to make certain assumptions: assumptions about what we need to have and what they need to have, assumptions about their attitude toward us and what ours ought to be toward them.

The closer our assumptions are to the way things are, the clearer it will be what it is that we will need to do to get what we want in the negotiation.

Inaccurate assumptions can kill an otherwise potentially mutually beneficial negotiation and relationship.

Here is a true story about a young boy named Billy.

NONE OF US SEES REALITY THE SAME.

CHECKING IN

Billy was a ten-year-old fifth-grader who had a small yard and gardening business he conducted after school and on the weekends. One Saturday morning, Billy was in Harold's barbershop waiting to get a haircut. Harold was still busy with a customer, so Billy went over to the telephone and made the following telephone call.

"Hello, Mrs. Anderson," he said. "I am a fifth-grader, and I have a lawn and garden care service that I do after school and on the weekends, and I was just wondering, Mrs. Anderson, if you would like me to take care of your lawn and garden?" "Oh, you already have someone doing that for you." "Oh, you are very satisfied with their work!" "Oh, and you are not thinking about making a change." "Oh, well, thank you for your time, Mrs. Anderson," and he hung up the phone.

Harold had overheard the conversation and said to Billy, "Billy, I thought you took care of Mrs. Anderson's lawn and garden."

"I do," said Billy. "I was checking in to check out how well I was doing."

Here we have, in this real-life case, a ten-year-old youngster who didn't just assume things were going well with his customers. He checked in to check out how well he was doing.

Anything that we assume to be true because we were born into a certain family, city, state, or nation and are

Check Out What Is Happening

identified with certain philosophical, religious, political, economic, social, or business traditions and institutions is a prejudice and discriminatory, and is and should be questioned. We live in a world with others—others who have vastly different views and perceptions of the way things are.

A study conducted by Bryant Wedge, a psychiatrist specializing in international studies, looked at the negotiation process between the United States and the then Soviet Union. His findings, although not totally unexpected, were rather disturbing. He found that the Russian and American negotiators held dramatically different views and assumptions about people, issues, and reality. These assumptions governed the way both sides negotiated. Yet neither the Americans nor the Russians checked in to check out their assumptions.

As M. Scott Peck comments on this study in his book *The Road Less Traveled*, "The inevitable result was that the negotiating behavior of the Russians seemed to the Americans to be either crazy or deliberately evil, and of course the Americans seemed to the Russians equally crazy or evil."

Doing business today is certainly rapidly becoming more global. We read about international mergers and strategic alliances in our daily newspapers. Seminars and conferences are given on how to conduct business with the Japanese, Chinese, Africans, and the rest of the world.

What happens in Beijing, China, or Tokyo, Japan, can well affect business practices in Iowa, USA. Businesses are becoming more global in nature, and national boundaries are becoming less distinct and perhaps even less important.

It will be increasingly incumbent on the world's negotiators, whether in the religious, social, political, economic, or business arena, to be like Billy and check in to check out how well things are progressing.

We assume that what we gave someone to do, got done; we assume that others are pleased with our work; we assume that the group understood our instructions; we assume that we have agreements that are mutually understood by others, including our family, friends, co-workers, boss, clients. We assume that somebody is doing a certain thing, but are they?

Does "Whose job is it?" strike a familiar chord?

*This is a story about four people named
Everybody, Somebody,
Anybody, and Nobody.
There was an important job to be done
and Everyone was asked to do it.
Everyone was sure Somebody
would do it.
Anybody could have done it,
but Nobody did it.
Somebody was angry about that,
because it was Everybody's job.
Everyone thought Anybody could do it
but Nobody checked in to check out that
Somebody was doing it.
It ended up Everybody blamed
Somebody when Nobody did what
Everybody thought had been done.*

Out of Everybody, Somebody, Anybody, and Nobody, no one checked in to check out what was really happening. They all assumed that the job was being done, but of course it wasn't.

All of us have seen how even the simplest communication can go astray. We thought we had an agreement, but we found that the other party didn't think so. We thought we did not have an agreement, but the other party believed we did have one.

CHECK OUT WHAT IS HAPPENING

Don't assume the other party sees the issues the same way you do.

"I thought … you thought … they thought … we thought." But I, you, they, and we thought wrong. It happens far too often in all aspects of our lives, doesn't it?

On important issues, check them out. Check out your assumptions to see how valid they are. To keep the negotiations moving in a spirit of goodwill and clarity, the successful negotiator checks in to check out the real status of important issues and agreements. The language of checking in to check out may be something as simple as:

➤ "Bill, this is Rob. I just wanted to check in with you to make sure that we are in agreement on how to proceed with the Sorenson account."

➤ "Bill, would you tell me what you see as our agreement on the Halverson contract?"

➤ "Susan, just checking in to see if there is anything you need for me to close the Williams account."

How many of us at times, sometimes critical times, assumed too much and then had our assumptions proven false?

In negotiating, this kind of checking in and checking out can prevent misunderstandings and mistakes before they happen. It can avoid confusion, resentment, and deadlock down the road. There is no assurance that checking in and checking out will gain you the agreement you want. But it will certainly help in keeping you on track toward agreement and enhance the spirit of your everyday negotiations.

Little Billy had the common sense to check his assumption that Mrs. Anderson thought he was doing a good job of taking care of her lawn. That job was important to Billy. He didn't take Mrs. Anderson's employment for granted.

We could benefit by following Billy's example and check out some of our important assumptions. Assumptions about how well we are doing for a particular important client, what the other party understood that we said about the concession we offered them, and on it goes.

> *The mediocre people who apply themselves go further than the superior people who don't.*
> —Baltasar Gracian

17

THOSE WHO IMPLANT SUGGESTIONS GOVERN THOSE WHO RECEIVE THEM

ALL THINGS WANTED in a negotiation do not have to be, nor should they be, a result of a direct demand, request, or proposal. In fact, statements like "I want," "I have to have," "I must have," "You will need to give me the following," "We need this and also that to close this deal" get very tiresome very quickly.

A suggestion does not invite a negotiation. Suggestions carry more of a collaboration, a partnering, a "Let's do it together" without a lot of debate, hassling, dickering back and forth, or bargaining. It is simply a recommendation, a proposal, a way of getting something done, without a lot of back-and-forth involved.

For example, "How would it be if we were to break for lunch now?" or "I would suggest that we table the following and leave it for the next group to negotiate," or "Why don't we simply let accounting work the numbers out for us, or leave it to the finance committee?" Suggestions can be either direct or indirect.

A direct suggestion might be something like "Why don't we go to Marjorie's Mexican Restaurant this evening? It is nearby, has great atmosphere, the food is out of this world, and the price is affordable." If you were

THROUGH SUGGESTION WE OFTEN GET WHAT WE WANT WITHOUT NEGOTIATING.

into negotiating instead of simply suggestion, you might say something like "I would like to negotiate with you where we eat tonight; I propose going to Marjorie's Mexican Restaurant."

Or the suggestion can more often be couched as an indirect suggestion, such as "You know, I read in the dining section of the newspaper that Marjorie's is rated Number 1 as the best local Mexican restaurant for the dollar." Or, "I don't know what you think as a customer, but I had a customer who thought it incredibly important that the training take two days for the material to have a chance to really be absorbed."

Haven't we all known someone who, just by the way they suggested something—whether it was a place to go for dinner or an idea on how to write up an ad for a marketing campaign—it was a done deal? Everyone felt good about it—no debates, no long protracted discussion.

By paying attention to the power of suggestion, one can enhance their ability to get more of what they want without negotiating, debating, or bargaining for such.

> *The reasonable man adapts himself to the world; the unreasonable one persists in trying to adapt the world to himself. Therefore all progress depends on the unreasonable man.*
> —George Bernard Shaw

18

Ask! Have you ever thought how much you have lost in life by not asking?

IN NEGOTIATING (as in life), asking is central to getting what you want from the other party. Most other parties have failed Mind Reading 101. They don't know or care what you want until you ask them for it.

Asking has many different aspects as we relate to others. I may ask for what I want so the other party can choose whether to honor my demand or not. I may ask, "What do you guys want to get out of this negotiation?" "What do we have to do to get an agreement on this issue with you?" "What would happen if we were to do this and that; what would you be able to do for us in return?"

Recall just a few things you have lost in life by not asking: not asking for help when you needed it; failing to ask someone what they wanted from you to make your relationship with them better; failing to ask for a raise when you felt you deserved it and then turning sour on your job because your boss didn't give to you what you didn't ask for.

WHEN YOU DON'T ASK FOR WHAT YOU WANT, YOU USUALLY DON'T GET IT.

Think of the times in and out of the negotiation arena when you didn't express your needs, didn't ask why. Do any of these strike home and underscore the power of asking?

When you don't ask for what you want, you usually don't get it. Volunteers in life whose purpose it is to give you what you want but didn't ask for are in very limited supply. They're an extinct species, is closer to the truth.

Ask and you shall receive is advice as old as humankind, found in great books of wisdom from the beginning to the present. What is the reason, then, for not asking for what we want? Might it be lack of self-esteem; feeling the other person should know and give us what we want without our asking for it; feeling that it is not right to ask someone for something and wanting them to give it to us without our asking for it; feeling we don't deserve it (whatever "it" may be); too shy; believing it is greedy to ask for what you want or at least they—the other party—may see it as such; desire to be seen as a nice person, a nondemanding person, a person who is unassuming; ad infinitum and ad nauseum?

How many transactions have gone wanting—negotiations that would have been win-win for all parties but never took place because one party required the other to be mind readers? When that requirement came up short, the discussion was cut short and the opportunity for good for all was lost.

We fail to learn and grow when we don't ask. We fail to get what we want when we don't ask, too.

A general observation: Most people like to give to you what you ask of them if they can and if it doesn't cost them much or anything at all to do it. You don't need examples of this, as they abound in all aspects of our lives. Times when your vendor would have been more than willing to help you out by delivering the items earlier or

ASK FOR WHAT YOU WANT IN WAYS THAT OTHERS WANT TO GIVE YOU WHAT YOU ASKED FOR.

later than originally agreed to; when the hotel would have upgraded your room as you are a regular customer and had a tough day; when a company would have eliminated a late charge because you overlooked the payment one month; when another company would have been willing to give you better terms than standard because you asked for them.

"He who is afraid to ask ... is ashamed of learning," says an ancient proverb.

> *The greatest human temptation is to settle for too little.*
> —Thomas Merton

19

Agent and third party: no authority to say yes or no but can be your ally

A COMMON MISCONCEPTION that some people apply to all negotiations is: Don't negotiate with anyone who lacks the authority to make the deal. Although it often makes sense to heed that advice, there are times when it's best NOT to negotiate directly with someone who has the authority, but rather with the person with access to the one who does—and then make sure you get him or her on your side.

As my eldest son Ken would soon be moving to the D.C. area with his young family to begin a doctoral program at Georgetown University, he and I went apartment hunting over a period of several days. Finally, he found "his" apartment. It was exactly what he wanted for his family. The panoramic views of the Potomac River, the Lincoln and Washington Memorials and the Capitol were awesome. The only problem was that the unit was going to come on the market a week after it had been cleaned up, and the agent was sure it would rent immediately. I concurred.

It was near the end of June, and Ken wouldn't be moving until mid-August. So how would we work to

AT TIMES IT IS BETTER TO NEGOTIATE WITH SOMEONE WHO HAS NO AUTHORITY.

The key to working with an agent or third party is to be sure that they are on your side.

negotiate this agreement? Some background information: The owner was a Georgetown University graduate, now living in Japan. The tenant had just moved out, sacked the apartment, and skipped paying the owner more than three months' rent.

I said to the agent showing us the apartment, "We will take the apartment, although we think the rent is just a little high, but that is acceptable. And the carpet certainly is in real need of replacement, but that is okay, too. And, of course, you understand that my son Ken will need to have the rent start the fifteenth of August when he moves here to go to the university.

Now you know, as I know, what the agent was going to say.

"Well, my owner can't hold the apartment that long, because I can have it rented by the first of July."

That was most likely true. But he would have had to show the apartment again—maybe several times before finding a qualified renter. Even then he would be taking a chance.

"I certainly can appreciate that, but you know my son is also a property owner as well as having been a tenant. He knows how to take care of property. And his wife is an immaculate housekeeper. The rent check will be deposited in the owner's bank account before it is due each month. Like the owner did, my son will attend Georgetown and may even be a senator or the president one of these days."

Now comes my closing question. "And of course you will be recommending to the owner that he accept Ken's offer to rent, won't you?"

The apartment became deathly silent. You know that kind of silence—it roars. The agent looked at me, then at Ken, then at the floor, and then out the window. Probably thinking, "Now, I don't want to be having to show this apartment next week instead of selling property, which is my real job. I have first and last month's rent in cash, in hand. Clearly this is a fine youth, and I can clear his references in hours. Maybe the kid will be president one day …"

He turned to my son and said, "Yes, I will recommend to the owner that he accept your offer."

We then knew it was a done deal. The next day the leasing papers were signed and the apartment rented, starting on the fifteenth of August. Generally, negotiate only with those whose authority holds solid truth. But there will be times, as in this case, when that will be impossible to do or even inadvisable to do. In the above apartment case, just the fact that the owner was in Japan would be enough to deter one.

Take the example cited in this lesson. At first glance it might have seemed better to have negotiated directly with the owner. But would the owner have accepted this wait period of nearly two months when the apartment could have most likely been rented quickly after being cleaned up? Probably not. But with the agent there, the owner can vent to the agent, argue that it doesn't make any sense to rent the apartment and hold it open for a couple of months. In turn, the agent can point out that both of them, the owner and the prospective renter, will have attended Georgetown University, that Ken is clearly responsible, married, that he would be putting down first and last months' rent, not asking for new carpet (which the apartment needed!), and not trying to get the monthly rent down.

The key to working with an agent or third party is to make sure they are on your side, genuinely want to put the deal together, and have the mind-set of a deal maker, not a deal breaker.

Anyone can find something to argue about in making any deal: It's not the right time; something better may come along; we don't know what the future will

WHEN NEGOTIATING, KNOW WHO HAS THE AUTHORITY TO MAKE THE DEAL.

bring; we don't know the full 100 percent implications of agreeing to this negotiation arrangement; we don't have all the facts to make the best decision; we might not get what we expect; the other party might not live up to their part of the agreement … and on and on it can go.

When entering the negotiation, know who has the authority to consummate the deal. If that information is not available at first, find out fast. Whether or not you work directly with the person in authority depends on the circumstances. There are situations exactly opposite in nature to the one cited here. In these cases, you only want to negotiate with the person who has the authority.

> *If you focus on people's shortcomings and forget about their strengths, then it will be hard to find worthy people in all the world.*
> —Taoist saying

20

Getting unstuck from a stuck negotiation

Mr. Carlson, an elderly retiree from Alaska, had moved to Santa Barbara, California, having fallen in love with the area. He purchased a small, five-unit apartment building near the beach and lived in one unit and rented the others out. He soon discovered that he didn't care to be a landlord and to have to deal with all the inevitable tenant problems and keeping up the property.

In fact, he hated tenants, and now when one of the units became available, he wouldn't even rent it. But neither would he hire professional management to help him.

Four years later he had had it with the property and was highly motivated to sell. Then he and his wife would be free to travel in their camper van around the country, visiting friends, relatives, and new places of interest and spending their years of remaining life doing what they loved to do.

He put a $400,000 price on the property, a good $85,000 over the market value. He was adamant about the price. It was nonnegotiable. He meant it when he said that he would never sell it for one penny less, even after he admitted it was way overpriced.

One day I asked, "Mr. Carlson, why do you insist on demanding $400,000 for your apartments when you know, I know, and anyone who would be a buyer would

Most reasons for getting stuck in getting from No to Go can be overcome.

WHEN STUCK, GO BEHIND THE POSITION TO DISCOVER THE REAL ISSUES FOR DEADLOCK.

know it is at least $85,000 overpriced? You want to spend your remaining years traveling around the country, visiting friends and relatives and enjoying yourself, free from owning this building. Why do you insist on $400,000?"

He said, "Rob, I am glad you asked. Because four years ago I bought the property for $400,000. I know property values have not gone up much since that time, and I admit I paid too much for the apartment even then. But having paid $400,000 for the property, all cash, my wife and children would not give me one day's rest if I sold it for less than I paid for it. Which again was $400,000. That is why I have to get $400,000 for the apartments, or I will die in this building before I would sell it for any less. Do you understand?"

"Yes, I do understand, Mr. Carlson. Before I tell you if I can sell your building for $400,000, I need to know. Would you consider taking a smaller property in trade as part of the purchase price and then taking back a loan for the remaining part?"

"Yes, if you get me my asking price" (which of course was $400,000, $85,000 overpriced). I then knew I would sell Mr. Carlson's property in a matter of days. And I did, and he got $400,000 for the property.

How did that happen, when Mr. Carlson was stuck in his position of demanding $400,000 for his apartment house, which was way overpriced? He had been trying to sell it for nine months before this. How did we get past his No to Go in selling his property? How was this accomplished in less than three weeks. Magic? No, actually it was fairly simple. We went behind the position of "I have to have $400,000" and looked at Mr. Carlson's needs, fears, wants, hopes, concerns. Although there was only one position—Carlson's $400,000 demand position—there were a multitude of fears, wants, needs, hopes, and concerns that Carlson had that could be addressed. Some of them could be negotiated.

Get behind the position and get to the core issues and concerns driving the position and see if they can be negotiated—as they were in the Carlson case.

Carlson wanted to travel and was concerned he was getting older and might miss out on this.

He didn't want to be criticized, perhaps even ridiculed, by his family for selling for less than he had paid for the units. He needed to save face and tell the world that he had not taken a loss on the property. He was willing to help finance the building and take a trade-in to help get the price he demanded.

All of these things were open to negotiation, whereas his position of $400,000 for his apartment units was not.

All of us face impasses and deadlocks in our negotiations. It comes with the turf. What to do when no give-and-take is taking place? When there is no agreement because one or more of the parties are stuck in their position?

Suspend the position. Stop talking about "I have to have this or that" and go behind the position and look at the concerns and wants, fears and issues important to the parties.

These inevitably are more negotiable and manageable than an unmovable position like Carlson's $400,000. An excellent book that speaks more fully to this issue of getting behind the position is *Getting to Yes,* by Roger Fisher and William Ury, based on their work with the Harvard Negotiating Project. It's well worth reading.

As I said, no magic was worked to get Carlson his price. Carlson accepted a small duplex in trade. Its current fair market value was $80,000, and it was traded to Carlson at $115,000. That was $35,000 of the $85,000 that needed to be accounted for. Then Carlson took back a note and trust deed for the remaining $285,000 at no interest for two and a half years, and then 7.5 percent interest for the remaining fifteen years. It was a good deal for the buyer, who had a duplex and wanted a larger unit near the beach. It was excellent for Carlson, as he got his

IF DEADLOCK OCCURS, GO BEHIND THE POSITION TO THE CONCERNS.

asking price (which was nonnegotiable to him) of $400,000 and was free to travel and do the things he felt he couldn't do as long as he owned the five units.

In any human dealing of importance, there are concerns, fears, wants, hopes, and understandings that go behind or, if you will, stand behind any negotiating position. If the position becomes one of deadlock, go behind the position to ascertain why. Is it an emotional issue, as in the case of Mr. Carlson? Is it one of distrust of the other party? Is it simply a case of misunderstanding that can be cleared up and the deadlock broken, so that a mutually satisfying agreement can be reached? What are the ego issues involved? Does one of the parties feel it is being taken advantage of or not being given enough credit or understanding? Setting aside or putting on hold the intractable positions of each party and then going behind them to find the whats, whys, and wherefores will enable you to negotiate agreements that on the surface looked as if there was no chance for them ever to happen.

Going behind the stuck position does not always break the deadlock. But it almost always, at a minimum, tells the parties the why of the deadlock and why there is not going to be an agreement. That has its own value.

> *There is always an easy solution to every human problem—neat, plausible, and wrong.*
> —H. L. Mencken

21

Trust is powerful— use it wisely

WHEN YOU TRUST SOMEONE, you have faith that they will do what they say they will do. You rely on them and have a certain dependence on such reliance in your relationships with them.

In many of our negotiating workshop sessions, we have the participants negotiate in a Blue-Green exercise that deals with trust and how one defines winning. Built into the exercise is a way in which both parties can come out with 72 points and win-win, or one party can try to take advantage of the other party, which almost always leads to fewer positive points for each party.

In the eight moves that the game affords, on the last move, one party could take advantage of the other by gaining one more positive point to 73 and causing the other party to lose 10 points and end up with a 62 instead of a 72.

One of the lessons in the exercise is to give the participants a chance to see how they view and handle the issue of trust.

In one of these exercises, when the eight short Blue and Green games moves had been completed and the scores tallied, one team looked visibly upset.

"What's the problem?" I asked.

"Well, you said that we could not talk on the first move, so we wrote the other team a note and said, 'If we

GUARD YOURSELF AGAINST UNTRUSTWORTHY PEOPLE.

You can trust the other party to do what it is best for them to do.

both go the plus 9 plus 9, then each team after the eight moves will earn plus 72 for Blue and plus 72 for the Green team. If you agree, sign the note.' And they signed the note, but on the last move those rascals gave us a minus 10 and they took a plus 10. And we ended up with 62 and they got plus 73."

I turned to the team that had done this dastardly act and said, "Well, what about it, guys? What happened?"

"What do you mean, what happened," they said.

"Well," I said, "you agreed to go plus 9 plus 9 win-win so both teams could end up with optimum scores of plus 72 plus 72, and then on the last move you took advantage of them. What about that?"

"Well," they responded, "we lie a lot." And that was it.

There are people in this world who will lie to you. There are people who are untrustworthy and against whom you have to guard yourself in any dealing you might have with them. Why, then, would one think it would be any different in a negotiation?

There was one other time I can recall, when doing this Blue-Green game, that the issue of trust was approached in a unique and creative way.

One team raised their hands just after the start of the exercise. "We don't trust each other," they said.

I looked at both teams, and I had to agree. They didn't look very trustworthy. So we entered into an agreement, and they took out two plastic bags from the hotel. One they marked "Blue team" and the other "Green team." The Blue team put all their wallets, cash, keys, credit cards, and watches into the Blue plastic bag, and the Green team did likewise with their wallets, watches, cash, and credit cards—put them into the Green plastic bag.

"We have agreed that if one team breaks trust and does a bad turn to the other team, the team wronged gets to keep all of the watches, wallets, rings, jewelry, and credit cards of the other team as a penalty for not living up to their agreement to go plus 9 plus 9 to win-win plus 72 for the Blue team and plus 72 for the Green team."

I had never seen anything like that before nor have I since. Of course, you know the results of that Blue-Green exercise: Both teams got plus 72.

Now, one might argue that this is not trust. Call it what you will, it certainly got the job done.

I took that idea and later implemented it when I negotiated a sale of some land in Santa Barbara, California, that I had subdivided. A builder wanted to develop a condominium complex on the land. We agreed to price and basic terms. Then I said, "You will need to put $25,000 into the California escrow before you begin to do any work on the property."

He said, "Rob, you don't trust me."

I responded that it wasn't necessarily an issue of trust, it was simply good business practice and doing due diligence. That made the deal, and it went very well. (It is considered one of the nicest condominium developments of its kind in Santa Barbara today.)

Trust is not absolutely necessary in negotiating; it can be considered the lubrication that makes a negotiation go so much more smoothly and easily. When one doesn't trust another in negotiating, everything becomes a struggle. Agreements, issues, and give-and-take that in a normal kind of negotiation would have been a no-brainer, in a negotiation without trust become major difficulties that cause struggling, questioning, and challenging.

You can trust the other party. That is, you can trust the other party in the negotiation to do what they think is the best thing for them to do. If they think the best thing for them to do is to be forthright and open with you, that is what they will do. If they think it is to their interest and advantage to lie to you, and they think they can get away with it, trust them to lie.

TRUST IS POWERFUL

So we face the challenge in our negotiating to set up the kinds of conditions and circumstances by which it is in the best interests of the parties to trust and to act in honest and fair ways with each other in the pursuit of gaining a win-win agreement that mutually benefits all involved.

Sometimes it will be necessary to put up some sort of collateral in case of default. We all have seen that when we have applied for secured loans for our business or home. Although the lender may argue that it is not a matter of trust, they aren't going to trust you to make the payments on those loans without proper collateral in case you default.

> *I know God will not give me anything I can't handle. I just wish He didn't trust me so much.*
> —Mother Teresa

22

When you change your mind, let the other party know why

Negotiating is the process of exchange. It is giving and taking in an effort to meet the needs of the parties. When you make a concession—that is, when you accommodate the other party or change your position, which is really changing your mind—let the other party know WHY you changed your mind. Why you made a concession or an accommodation that changed your position. If you don't, they will think that you are lying to them.

Let's create a situation where you are selling your grand piano because you are retiring and moving into a smaller condominium. You run an ad in the local newspaper advertising your grand piano for $3,500. An interested party has come to the house, likes the piano, but feels $3,500 is too high. You talk a while and then say to him, "Okay, you can have it for $3,000."

A cardinal rule in negotiating is never to make a concession without making it conditional. The condition assures you that you will not give something for nothing. It protects the concession and gives value to the concession. The condition is, in a sense, the price tag that the other party must meet in order to get what is being offered. In this case the piano is being offered.

Without trust, everything is a struggle.

IN NEGOTIATING, NEVER MAKE A CONCESSION WITHOUT MAKING IT CONDITIONAL ON GETTING SOMETHING IN RETURN.

In the above example, though, more than one negotiation principle has been violated. When you said, "Okay, you can have it for $3,000," that was very bad negotiating. There is no condition placed on the concession—a major violation. Second, there is no explanation of why you moved from $3,500 to $3,000. You have changed your mind and position from $3,500 to $3,000. Why? If you don't give an explanation, the other party will think that you lied to them. First you said that you had to have $3,500 for the grand piano, and now you are telling them that you will take $3,000—without offering an explanation.

There may be situations where it would not be in your best interests to tell the true motivating reason you are selling, say, your grand piano. You are moving to a smaller home, the children are all grown, and there is simply no space or any particular interest in hauling a grand piano along in your senior years.

There may be times when you do not want the other party to know the real motivation for your making the concession. Let's say, for example, it is Saturday morning. You have been advertising and showing the grand piano in your home for over two weeks, and no one has purchased it.

Your spouse has had it with trying to sell the piano. She wants no more of it, and says in her special and wonderful way, "Dear, I have had it with your trying to sell this grand piano and having strangers come into our home, interrupt our lives, trying to sell the darn thing. If you don't sell this piano by 6:00 P.M. tonight, I will get an ax and chop this piano into kindling wood or at least my half of the piano."

It is now 2:30 P.M. on this fateful Saturday afternoon. Now, do you want to tell the other party this bit of vital information? For instance, "Well, Harold, I appreciate your coming over to the house this afternoon and for showing an interest in buying this wonderful grand piano advertised for $3,500. By the way, Harold, I want you to know something. If I don't sell this grand piano by this afternoon, my wife is going to chop it into kindling wood. As that is in less than four hours, Harold, please make me an offer."

Perhaps Harold will take pity on you and say, "You seem like such a nice guy, and I want to help you out in this tough situation, so I will buy your piano and not only give you the $3,500 that you are asking for it but $1,000 more for being really honest with me, buddy." Highly unlikely.

One question that might come to mind is: "How honest do I have to be with the other party?"

What do you mean by "honest?" If by "honest" you mean that you have to tell all, be frank and candid, and let them know your innermost feelings, concerns, wants, fears, and personal data, no. Not when it's none of their business.

This is a personal opinion, but it's shared by many: You and I have no responsibility or obligation to tell anyone the truth, if it is none of their darn business.

Does that mean that you tell the truth? Depends on what is meant by "truth." You might want to discuss this concept of honesty with the other party before and during your negotiations.

One might ask, "Can't one just assume they know the reason why I made the concession?"

Sure, you can assume that, but at best you'd better check in to check out if your assumptions are valid. This also gives you the opportunity to build a strong rationale and conditions for giving the concession. This dialogue with others can be beneficial to both parties. Don't get in the "they should have known" business unless that makes your life work better for you.

Now, how should one respond if the other party were to ask directly, "What is the real reason you are selling your piano?" How do you answer this direct question?

MOST PEOPLE HAVE FLUNKED MIND READING 101.

CHANGING YOUR MIND

NEVER MAKE A CONCESSION WITHOUT MAKING IT CONDITIONAL.

A master negotiator seeks balance in all that is done. What is the proper balance between telling the "whole truth" and a select version of it? I personally believe I have no obligation to tell anyone the truth! That is, I don't have to tell anyone the truth if it is none of their business.

There is truth about my personal relationship with my wife that is no business of anybody's except my wife and me. Then, in that case, if someone were to ask me a personal question about my love life with my wife, I have no obligation to tell them the truth. Does that mean that I can lie to them? No, but I don't have to tell them the truth.

In our scenario here, shouldn't I have let the other party make the first offer and said to Harold, "What will you give me for my grand piano?"

There are two schools of thought on the subject of who should make the first offer. You may have heard the saying, "He who speaks first, loses, or she who makes the first offer, loses."

Just the opposite can happen when done correctly. We might say, "In the spirit of gaining a win-win agreement, we are willing to do the following and make the first offer. We can do it if you will accommodate us in the following ways."

Your BOON (Best Option Outside Negotiation) in the case of selling your piano was bleak, to say the least. You could have called the Salvation Army or your favorite charity that could use a grand piano. You could have told them to be at your house no later than 5:00 P.M. to pick up the piano. Perhaps their statement that they would pick it up, but not until Wednesday, their regular pickup day, might have assuaged your spouse.

You might have arranged to have your neighbor take the piano off your hands in exchange for something. You might have arranged for a late-afternoon auction. All bids accepted, no bid too low. There are almost always alternatives, some better than others. One mistake is to assume that there are no alternatives.

Remember that there are many roads that can lead from No to Go. We can almost always create additional options to what we currently see as the best option. One of those alternative options may prove to be the one that should be taken. Rightly changing position, demands, concessions, and strategies are all part of gaining a desired agreement with others.

> *You must pay the price if you wish to secure the blessing.*
> —Andrew Jackson

23

AFTER THE DEAL IS SIGNED, IT STILL ISN'T OVER

For years now I have given out a wallet-size plastic card listing "The Master Plan for Successful Negotiators" to people at our negotiating seminars, colleagues, and clients, and have used this card as my business card. Many have kept this card in their wallet or purse as a constant reminder of ways to successful negotiations. Some have attested that just before they have entered into a particularly important negotiation they have taken out the card and reviewed its salient, powerful points inscribed on both sides of the card.

Under the caption "After the Negotiation" are listed five key points to keep in mind:

1. *Get clear, signed agreements.* Put your agreements and conditions in writing. It will give a degree of importance and seriousness to any negotiation, in contrast to a nonwritten agreement. It gives the parties an opportunity to scrutinize and to review what the understandings are.

2. *Reaffirm value.* The whole purpose of the negotiation is to increase value for each party. The aim is to be better off for having negotiated than for not having negotiated. In this step it is important for all parties to first affirm the value they each received and then to reaffirm the value the other party received.

YOU CAN LOSE THE NEGOTIATION EVEN AFTER IT IS SIGNED.

We all at times have had second thoughts about something we have agreed to do or not to do. Probably more than one person has had doubts after purchasing that car that exceeded the family budget or an extra smart-looking but quite expensive sweater, or after entering into an agreement to take on a project, to get married, to contribute financially to a particular nonprofit fund, and so on.

To affirm something is to declare it, to warrant it, to assert it. In this case, reaffirming the value received from the negotiation proclaims the wisdom of the agreement. It makes public (although not necessarily announced to the world) that the right course of action was taken by both parties to advance their respective best interests.

3. *Maintain good relationships.* To keep up good relationships, acknowledge the worth of each party and their special honored relationship now that the deal is closed. Change is constant. Expect circumstances to come up that will necessitate midcourse adjustments and probably renegotiations in part or in whole of the agreements made today. Keeping open communications and establishing and exhibiting trust supports superior relationships. It is amazing how easy it is to leave what was a good solid relationship at the beginning to be taken for granted. Count on missing out on the positive things that might have been if the relationship had been attended to properly and opportunistically. I strongly suspect that if as much time were devoted to carrying out relationships as the time and effort expended to start a new relationship, the world would be a better place for all of us.

A classic example of this is how we courted our future spouse. How sensitive we were to their needs, how eager we were to please, how much time we took to listen, to be interested, to really care about them. And

WHEN THE DEAL IS OVER, ALL PARTIES WANT TO FEEL GOOD ABOUT IT.

then what happened to that negotiated relationship—your marriage—ten, fifteen, twenty years later?

Take your working relationship with your secretary or your assistant. How much time and effort are you investing in keeping that "negotiated relationship" up to par and exceeding par, if you will?

None of us wants to be taken for granted. We want to be acknowledged for our worth and for the contributions we make to ongoing relationships. Maintaining and increasing the value of the relationship takes creativity, commitment, skill, some good fortune, and lots and lots of just plain hard work. Is it worth that investment to maintain the relationship? That is a judgment call each of us has to make for ourselves. Some never even really give it much thought and lose out on all the good things that might have been if just a little more commitment had been made to the relationship.

4. *Reinforce the mutual benefits.* Here I mean not only to acknowledge value received, but especially the mutual benefits received by each party and how they may not only be supported but, when feasible, enhanced. If I have purchased an extensive office computer system, the service support people might not only affirm that I made the right choice, but as time proceeds they undoubtedly will be able to show me ways that I can make even better use of the products and of their accompanying benefits to me. These might be benefits that I had not even seen at the time the deal was put together and agreed upon.

5. *Prepare for future negotiations.* Unless we are dealing with a onetime kind of deal, prepare for future negotiations. Studies and common sense tell us that it is easier and often more profitable to pay attention to the customers and relationships we have now. Knowing that the chances are good that you

will be having to work with the parties in the future, then maintaining clear agreements, reaffirming value, and maintaining good working relations to reinforce the mutual benefits will go a long way toward making future negotiations happen, and happen with results in the way we desired.

Nearly all important relationships of more than sixteen minutes are negotiated relationships. (You can use any number of minutes, hours, or days you wish, but sixteen minutes sounds just about right.) Of these, one of the most important for millions of people is marriage. Marriages would be greatly bolstered and strengthened if the partners were to take to heart the principle of managing the negotiation after the wedding ceremony and the honeymoon period are so much history. It is so very easy to take the other party for granted in and out of marriage, at work, and at home. Don't do that.

Closing the deal is the opening of another stage of an ongoing give-and-take. Manage it well.

You can observe a lot by watching.
    —Yogi Berra

24

YOU AND OTHERS—HOW PEOPLE TREAT YOU IN THE NEGOTIATION

PEOPLE ARE THE MOST important ingredient in any effort to get from No to Go. Certainly the issues are central, the timing can play an important role, and so can the environment, but people make things happen or not. To fail to give the proper attention to the people aspect of any negotiation is the direct passport to failure.

In life we generally train others how to treat us, and it is no different in the negotiating arena. How we perceive ourselves may be different from how others perceive us, but we start with ourselves.

In regard to being a successful negotiator, if I see myself as one who does not deserve all the good things that can come from a successful negotiation, then that is probably what I will end up with. That is far less than what I could have and should have received for the negotiation process. Be in the business of supporting yourself.

When you enter into the negotiation, the other side will instinctively and even methodically size you up. They will take in an impression of you in terms of your confidence in getting what you want; your passion for

> **PEOPLE ARE APT TO ACCEPT YOUR JUDGMENT ABOUT YOURSELF UNTIL YOU PROVE THEM WRONG.**

the transaction; your skill, background, motivations, and validity of your positions; and your options and alternatives within and without the negotiations.

You never have a second chance of making a first impression. What you say, how you conduct yourself, the way that you listen, speak, move, and overall generally present yourself, will in part affect what you get.

Let's revisit the statement that people generally treat you the way that you have trained them to treat you—in any relationship. In part this follows the general pattern that others, in this case the people you are negotiating with (and we note that it is people we are negotiating with, even when those people represent some large monolithic organization), will generally accept your judgment about yourself, unless you give them reasons to do otherwise.

If you believe that you have the right to ask for something in the negotiation and do so, the other side will generally accept that you have this right. (It doesn't mean, of course, that they will give you what you asked for.) If you act in ways that send the message to them that you don't really have the right to what you are asking for, they will also generally accept that as so (and, in this case, most assuredly will not give it you, unless it serves their own self-interest).

So, what are some implications of this for improving your negotiating success? First, look the part that fits best with what you are trying to get out of the negotiation. If that means that you take a very proactive role, so be it. If that means that you need to be more laid back in your approach—perhaps doing more active listening, questioning for additional information, being less aggressive, biding your time—so be it.

You are playing a role, the role of a successful negotiator. Your persona needs to reflect that particular role. You will know better what the role is in relationship to your counterparts when you have done your homework

BEWARE OF "AFTER DEAL" REMORSE.

and understand where they are coming from, what their negotiation styles are like, and what their general approach is to negotiating with you.

Remember, your counterpart is not Mother Teresa. They are not in the negotiation to make sure you get the best deal possible. Their allegiances are not to you, or they would be sitting on your side of the table (figuratively if not literally).

Do not look to others to do what you should do for yourself. You and you alone are responsible for taking care of yourself. Always keep in mind what the role of the other side is. It is not a binding fiduciary relationship to you—to work to their best advantage, even if it means putting their interest second, to get you the best for you.

The second thing to remember is that they have their own frame of reference, meaning they have their own unique and self-serving point of view in a negotiation. How they see things makes perfectly good sense to them; therefore it is perfectly justified in their minds. The power to rationalize one's actions is never ending and complete.

So don't look to them to do what you should do yourself, and recognize that you both have the same reality but may have two quite different views of that reality.

Third, be very wary of the man who carries the biggest Bible. He who talks a good game, who is going to do so much for you, who presents you with such a good deal it is hard to believe, probably shouldn't be believed.

Ask yourself: Who is this person, group, or organization that is so anxious to be my friend, my benefactor? And for what self-serving reasons do they come to this table and propose such? Carrying the biggest Bible does not mean they are the biggest believers in and adherents of the content of that Bible. Nor does the fact that they propose all these good things to you mean that is what they truly mean and can deliver to you. And of course, ask yourself at what cost are all these supposed good things coming to you.

On your road from No to Go, you will encounter all types of people you have to deal with. You cannot always control how they will treat you. You can, of course, control how you choose to feel about them. This choice often plays an important role in determining whether you will get from No to Go.

> *You can not control the natures of other people, but you can control how you'll deal with them.*
> —Harry Browne

Section IV

Rules & Caveats of Negotiating

25. Don't wobble—know what you want and negotiate to get it.

26. The other party wants to feel good about having negotiated with you.

27. Remember, in negotiating as in life, it isn't over till it's over.

28. Things are not always what they seem.

29. Know the other party's Best Option Outside Negotiation (BOON).

30. Don't make a deal so good that it is bad.

31. You do what you can do.

25

DON'T WOBBLE—KNOW WHAT YOU WANT AND NEGOTIATE TO GET IT

AS FRANK ENTERS the negotiation conference room, his walk, body language, speech, and overall demeanor indicate that he is scared, unsure of himself, unfocused, and generally in a state of mind and body wobbling. None of which, by the way, goes unnoticed by his negotiating counterparts.

We only get one chance to make a first impression. The impression Frank made conveyed all the wrong messages to his opponent. It was as if Frank carried an invisible around his neck that read: TAKE ADVANTAGE OF ME. HIT ME. I DON'T KNOW WHAT I WANT OR HOW TO GO ABOUT GETTING IT EVEN IF I DID. I AM CONFUSED, UNSURE, SCARED, AND VULNERABLE. I JUST WANT TO GET OUT OF HERE. I AM GOING TO LOSE. I AM NOT PREPARED AND SKILLED IN NEGOTIATING. I WILL DEFINITELY GET THE SHORT END OF THE STICK.

As we view this scene, we can just begin to imagine how the outcome will be for Frank and whom he is representing. Will the other party take advantage of Frank?

Knowing what we know about people and the way some see negotiating, would we be surprised to see Frank

THE KEY TO GETTING FROM NO TO GO IS DON'T WOBBLE.

FLEXIBILITY AND WOBBLING MIGHT LOOK SIMILAR BUT THEY ARE TOTALLY DIFFERENT.

making more concessions than he really needed to and should have? Or giving in to demands that were out of place and detrimental to his best interests? Would we be surprised to see the other side being far more demanding, far more aggressive, and far less willing to give and take?

All of these elements, and maybe more, work to Frank's disadvantage. Frank's wobbling is perceived as a weakness, that he is milk toast, not very smart, and deserves what he is getting (or not getting) in this particular negotiation.

The power of the human mind to rationalize, to justify what we do, is amazing. No less so for Frank's counterpart to rationalize what they did to him in this negotiation, due primarily to Frank's own wobbling and weaknesses.

Although we would like to believe that each party in a negotiation would display fairness and courtesy for all the others involved, it is not their principal responsibility to take care of Frank. It is their responsibility to take care of themselves. It might not be too surprising to find that they interpret taking care of themselves as taking and getting all they can get from Frank—by exploiting his vulnerability. We are, of course, saying that Frank has put himself in harm's way.

So don't wobble. If you find yourself doing so, request some time-out. Leave the negotiating area. Call for help.

The key lesson in negotiating from No to Go is, don't wobble. Know what you want and how to go about getting it in a focused, positive, purposeful, and skillful manner.

There is the story of a forest weasel who sat upon a rock and watched potential prey go by. All of a sudden, he would attack one and kill it. When asked, "Weasel, how do you determine which prey to strike and kill?" the weasel answered, "I just watch their walk. If they walk as if they don't know where they are going, and wobble, I move in for the kill and hit them."

As the weasel watched the potential prey walk by, he looked for weakness and vulnerability, for lack of purpose and direction. Instead of Mr. Weasel sitting on a rock, looking down at potential prey, imagine your Mr. Weasel, your counterpart, watching you. It's as simple as that. So don't wobble!

Our metaphoric weasel can sometimes take the human form of muggers. A TV talk-show host interviewed some ex-muggers ("ex" because they were now in jail). She asked them how they chose whom to mug out of all the possible victims walking on the streets of the city."

They replied that if a person's walk indicated they were scared and did not know where they were going, if they were indecisive and seemed confused, they hit them. On further questioning, they remarked they seldom would consider, let alone attack, an individual—regardless of age, sex, or size—if the person appeared confident, direct, and purposeful in their walk and where they were going.

A recent graduate of a law school joined a small law firm that specialized in criminal law. Part of her legal responsibilities was to interview and work with convicted criminals while they were in jail. She was frightened and evidently showed it. She said, "They could smell fear in my walk and talk, and that was scary. They knew—they knew I was scared."

This reminds me of the scene in the Academy Award–winning film *Silence of the Lambs.* Jodie Foster plays a young FBI agent attempting to interrogate the apprehended serial killer, Hannibal Lector, played by Anthony Hopkins. In this film, Hannibal could smell Foster's character's fear, and he worked to use it against her and to his advantage. So it will also be with our negotiating opposite if we give them the opportunity by wobbling.

During Operation Desert Storm in 1991, President George Bush faced far-reaching decisions about committing

WOBBLERS SELDOM GET FROM NO TO GO SUCCESSFULLY.

U.S. troops to act in Kuwait against the aggression of Saddam Hussein. Remarking on this situation, England's then prime minister, Margaret Thatcher, said to President Bush, relative to whether or not the United States should send troops to the war-stricken area, "George, don't wobble."

No matter how one might evaluate former President Bush, he did not, in this case, wobble.

When we don't know what we want and don't know how to go about getting it, and we sidestep issues, hesitate, and falter, we are wobbling. Don't do that in your serious negotiations (or, for that matter, in your whole life). Know what you want and go out to get it.

At first glance, flexibility and wobbling might look like kissing cousins. They might seem to be of a similar nature with just a fine line separating them. No. Flexibility is a valuable attitude and trait to have in striking the best negotiated deals, whereas wobbling does nothing but confuse, disorient, and subtract from the good that can come from a well-negotiated transaction.

Remember, the signals sent by the wobbler in a negotiation are: "I don't know what I want"; "I lack the commitment and focus in getting it"; "I am vulnerable; come and take advantage of me." Well, maybe not in so many words, but you get the picture.

Here are some specific ways to reduce and completely eliminate unwanted wobbling:

> **First,** write down what it is that you specifically must have out of a given negotiation.
>
> **Second,** rehearse and visualize asking for and getting what you want from the other party.
>
> **Third,** know what you are willing to pay to get what you want.

Fourth, have a well-thought-out Best Option Outside Negotiation (BOON) so you know where you are going to walk (or even run) to, but do not wobble if you don't get what you have to have from this particular negotiation.

There is an ancient Chinese saying: "When sitting, just sit. When standing, just stand. Above all, don't wobble."

> *Until one is committed, there is hesitancy, the chance to draw back, always ineffectiveness.... I have learned a deep respect for one of Goethe's couplets:*
>
> Whatever you can do, or dream you can, begin it. Boldness has genius, power and magic in it.
>
> **—W. H. Murray**

26

THE OTHER PARTY WANTS TO FEEL GOOD ABOUT HAVING NEGOTIATED WITH YOU

WHEN THE NEGOTIATION is over, both parties want to feel as if they got a good deal. The party with whom you've negotiated wants to feel that doing so was advantageous and that they are better off because of the negotiation. If they ever get the feeling they were taken advantage of, if they feel bad after the negotiation, and later they have the opportunity to get even with you, they probably will.

Party B made the following remarks after concluding a negotiation with Party A: "I felt we were taken advantage of. Those guys pushed us to the wall and could have been more accommodating than they were. They knew we were pressed for time, and they took advantage of our precarious position. There will be another day somewhere and somehow to even the score.

"There was a certain arrogance, a cavalier looking-down-their-noses at us that I resented. Although they gave on some issues, when they did, they did it in such a way as to intimate that they were doing us a great favor that we didn't deserve or earn, but that they would tolerate giving it to us out of the kindness of their heart.

"If we didn't need the deal so bad and if they didn't

EVERYONE WANTS TO FEEL LIKE THEY GOT A GOOD DEAL.

know we needed it so bad, I would say to hell with them. I can assure you that there will be a day when all this will return to haunt them."

These remarks show that Party B was not happy and felt they had been taken. It is one thing to negotiate a tough and hard deal. It is another thing to take unneeded advantage of the other party. This should be particularly clear when the one thing we know about negotiating with others is that they want to feel good about negotiation with us.

They (the other party, Party B) feel bad when:

➤ You as Party A got more than they (Party B) think you deserved. Note that it makes little difference to them if you really deserved what you got (certainly from your point of view, as Party A, you could easily believe you deserved what you got), or that they as Party B got a great deal. It is Party B's perception—that you got more than you deserved—that is the driving force; it may have nothing to do with what is right, fair, just, or even what is so.

Remedy: Make sure Party B doesn't feel this way. You as Party A might have to play down the advantages you are getting. You might need to show the other party that in fact you are not getting a better deal than you deserve from them. Show them what your BOON—that is, your Best Option Outside Negotiation—with them is and say that if you don't get at least that much from them as Party B, then you will terminate the negotiation and go to the other party, where you will get a better deal.

➤ They got less than they thought they deserved. This means that from their perspective, you as Party A cheated them in some way. It is interest-

GIVE THE OTHER PARTY THEIR "BRAGGING RIGHTS."

NEVER UNDERESTIMATE THE IMPORTANCE OF THE HUMAN DYNAMICS IN ANY GIVEN NEGOTIATION.

ing how each of us sees the world from a different perspective. You as Party A might think you are being extremely generous in your negotiating concession to Party B, but they don't see it that way at all. One of the challenges you face is to demonstrate to them the value of what they have received. It is possible they don't see all the good that might come from what they are getting from you. At least you might point out how much worse off they would be if they didn't conclude the negotiation with you, as you are their best deal.

➤ Their expectations were violated. One of the most common reasons why people get upset is that their valued expectations were violated. If they thought they deserved to get that job promotion at the office and it was given to someone else, they certainly will not be pleased, to say the least.

➤ They felt put down, embarrassed, or mistreated in some way and robbed of their bragging rights. It is entirely possible that Party A had little or no clue that their opposite (Party B) felt this way. After all, most of us flunked Mind Reading 101.

What makes the other party feel good? Some things are obvious, some not so obvious, and many are often overlooked when it would cost little or nothing to give them that good feeling.

They (Party B) feel good when:

➤ They have bragging rights. They can go back and tell whomever they need to that they got a good deal. They were tough, and although it was a tough negotiation, they came out winning. By giving them these "bragging rights" you give them the opportunity to feel good about the negotiation and, of course, about themselves.

You buy a car and you want to be able to tell your spouse, friends, or co-workers how you were able to get the dealer to come down on the price or how you got the salesperson to throw in car mats and a stereo radio for free or . . .

What is important is not what you got or didn't get. What is important is how you feel about it and how you can "justify" your buy, brag about it to whomever you feel you need to brag to. Then you can hear those sweet words, "Gee, Rob, you are a real tough negotiator. How did you do that? That was great. WOW." And on it goes. Do not underestimate the importance of giving the other party their bragging rights. That is just good human dynamics.

MAKE SURE THE OTHER PARTY DOES NOT FEEL YOU GOT MORE FROM THEM THAN YOU DESERVED.

➤ They are able to save face. In some negotiations it might be very difficult to give the other party many bragging rights, but at a minimum you can be sure that they can save face. You might arrange to have it seem that Party B took the initiative to negotiate the deal. You might give them more time to conclude the deal than usual, you might let them rescind part of the agreed-to contract, or you might reduce a demand as a concession to them.

➤ They can feel they were tough negotiators. Find something that you can compliment them on. "Boy, you guys certainly know how to negotiate to get what you want." "You guys were tough on that issue, fair but tough. I certainly wouldn't want to meet you in a dark alley."

TO GET FROM NO TO GO, BOTH PARTIES HAVE TO SEE A BENEFIT IN DOING SO.

- They feel that you (Party A) ended up with less than you would have with "less experienced" negotiators than themselves. This reinforces that they are pros and that some party with fewer skills and less knowledge, experience, savoir-faire, or power would have given you much more than they did. They can take pride in this accomplishment. They know how to negotiate.

- Party B feels that you (as Party A) didn't get more than you deserved. No matter how much Party B got from you (Party A), they don't want you to get more than you deserve. That may mean that at times, you as Party A must play down what you got. It certainly says be careful about how and whom you tell about what a fabulous deal you got from Party B, especially if what you got could in any way be interpreted as meaning Party B got less because of this.

What you can do to make the other party feel good about negotiating with you:

- They hear from a third party that Party A thought they were tough, experienced. Often if someone else who was not part of the negotiation tells them they were great, it has even more impact and is more believable than if Party A (you) tells Party B they were tough.

- They see the benefits to themselves for having concluded the negotiation. They realize the good things that are coming from the agreement. Party A (you) might simply review the outcome with them, anticipating all the good things that will be coming, the profits to be made, the additional business to be acquired.

> **WORK TO ENSURE THAT THE OTHER PARTY FEELS GOOD ABOUT THE AGREEMENT.**

- They get something extra that was not expected. They get an extra discount, extra time, a lower percentage rate, more orders than negotiated, a recommendation or referral not asked for, and so on.

- They feel they earned it. It seems that when we work hard for something, when we put out effort and skill and knowledge to work to get it, and we feel we earned it, then we respect and covet it more.

- They see others getting a worse deal than they got. "Great, look how much better a deal we got on our vacation plan than Roberts got." Human nature being what it is, we don't want others getting a better deal than we do, whether it's negotiating a better seat on the airplane or getting extra work done on the home by a contractor.

What are the benefits to you of ensuring that the other party feels good about having negotiated with you? No one does anything if they cannot see a benefit to themselves in doing it, at least at the time they do it. So what are the benefits to you of helping Party B feel good about negotiating with you as Party A? Some are obvious, some not so obvious.

- Less struggle. It just makes it a lot easier to do business with the other party when they feel good about you and the negotiated transaction.

- They might feel they owe you one. That depends on how you have set this up in the scheme of things.

- You have made a "friend" and ally. Anytime you can make them look good at little or no additional expense to you, you stand to gain much now and in the future.

➤ Goodwill. When the inevitable crunches come, obstacles present themselves, problems appear—and they will—you have the foundation of respect and goodwill that can be called upon to deal with the problems. Changes abound. Conditions change. What made sense yesterday might not make sense today and is certainly up for review tomorrow.

➤ They are easier and better to work with now and in the future.

➤ Future business.

➤ Developing a reputation that invites people to do business with you.

➤ You feel good.

Why do we forget to make the other party feel good? It's surprising how little attention is paid to making the other party feel good. Why is this?

➤ It takes time.

➤ It takes some sensitivity.

➤ It's easy to ignore or overlook the human part of the negotiation equation.

➤ They already know what a good deal they got.

➤ I shouldn't have to tell them.

➤ I assume they know.

➤ I don't care.

➤ It's not necessary. After all, we are all mature, professional, hardworking businesspeople, adults.

➤ If you tell them, they will want more; they'll think you are lying to them or playing up to them.

I shall pass through this world but once. Any good therefore that I can do or any kindness that I can show to any human being, let me do it now. Let me not defer or neglect it for I shall not pass this way again.

—Anonymous

27

Remember, in negotiating as in life, it isn't over till it's over

During the 1984 football season, I attended all the Navy games, as my son was co-captain of the Navy team. A couple of games in particular stand out in that standout season. One was at East Rutherford, New Jersey, where Navy had played Notre Dame hard. The score stood at Navy 17, Notre Dame 15, when the game gun went off—assuredly a tremendous victory for Navy. My son went over to the head referee to ask for the game ball, which is the prerogative of the winning team's captain.

Then an announcement was made over the public address system. The game clock was being put back by three seconds. It turned out to be just enough time to give Notre Dame the opportunity to kick a field goal and beat Navy by two points: 18 to 16.

The referee came over to my son, Eric, and said, "Son, did you learn anything today? It ain't over until it's over."

I don't know if the referee was quoting the famous Yogi Berra expression or not: "It isn't over till its over," but I didn't give a darn. I am still sick about that game as I write this.

In negotiation, much as in football, it isn't over until it's over, and even then it might not be over.

It isn't over till it's over.

108   From No to Go

We have all had times when we thought we had reached an agreement with our family, with our boss, with co-workers, vendors, or the like, only to find, most often to our dismay, that we were wrong. What we had thought was a done deal, wasn't.

How many times have even seasoned master negotiators left the negotiating table thinking that they had a deal, only to find out to their dismay that it was not true? They assumed that there was agreement on quality specification, on delivery time, on ability to make changes down the track, only to find out they were wrong.

Many a handshake on "It's a DEAL" turns out to be at best premature.

Check out your important assumptions. Do your due diligence and get the important stuff down in writing and not left to memory (memory pales in comparison to the weakest ink.)

> *The hardest thing to learn in life is which bridge to cross and which bridge to burn.*
> —David Russell

28

THINGS ARE NOT ALWAYS WHAT THEY SEEM

THERE ARE TIMES when negotiating a deal seems to be to good too be true. Maybe it is too good to be true. Someone seems to be very open to your suggestions, but in reality they have already made up their mind and you are the one who is going to lose.

You think you have an agreement but you don't. You think you understood what the other party said, but you didn't. You thought everything was okay, only to find out that was not the case at all.

You thought because the other person had their arms crossed and looked tough, they were going to be difficult to negotiate an agreement with. It turned out the exact opposite was true: They were very interested and easy to work with.

It is far too easy to jump to conclusions without checking things out carefully. Don't assume, and certainly when it is not to your advantage. Think what this may mean to you in your life negotiations.

Perhaps this next story will illustrate the point that things are not always what they seem …

When Pope John Paul came to Denver in 1996 to speak at a world youth celebration, the story was told that he had a few hours to spare before addressing the thousands of

BE SKEPTICAL. ASK QUESTIONS.

youths who had come to hear him speak. Visiting Denver for the first time, the Pontiff remarked to his chauffeur, "I would like to see some of Denver and the surrounding areas."

"Fine," responded his chauffeur, "if his Excellency will simply get in the back seat, we will be off."

"Oh, no," remarked the Pope. "I want to drive. It has been a long time since I last was behind the wheel of a car, so you get in the back and I will get in the front and drive."

With great reluctance the chauffeur got in the back seat, the Pope at the driver's wheel, and off they went. Within a short time, they were stopped by a police officer for running a red light. When the officer came up to the limousine, he looked in and saw whom he had stopped. He called in to his immediate supervisor in a near panic.

"Chief, I don't know what to do. I just stopped a most important person for running a red light. What should I do?"

"Well," his boss replied, "if he isn't the president or God, give him a ticket."

"Well, sir, he isn't the president, and I don't know if he is God or not, but his chauffeur is the Pope."

Again, it is so easy to jump to conclusions, to make judgments about things we do not have the full information on. It is all too easy to simply see what seems to be without asking, probing, or inquiring to further clarify and substantiate our impressions.

This story reminds us that things are not always as they seem. Be skeptical. Question. Make proper inquiries to clarify the matter at hand. There will inevitably be times when you will misread the intentions, state of mind, or purpose of your negotiating counterpart. It may be of little consequence, or it might cost you dearly for not having checked out your impressions and assumptions.

The following anonymous short scenario I have always

liked. It challenges me each time I read it to think about cause and effect, and to acknowledge to myself that things aren't always what they seem to be. Each of us brings a unique perspective to our individual worlds.

> *"Why are you standing here on this street corner wildly waving your hands and shouting?"*
> *"I'm keeping away the elephants."*
> *"But there aren't any elephants here."*
> *"You bet: That's why I'm here."*
> **—Anonymous**

29

Know the Other Party's Best Option Outside Negotiation (BOON)

A VICE PRESIDENT OF ONE of our local banks wanted the loan business of a large homebuilder in the area. When I talked with her, she lamented the fact that the bank had been unsuccessful in even getting the builder to come in and talk to the bank.

I asked her, "Phyllis, what seems to be the problem?"

She answered, "I don't know."

"Where is he now banking, and what kind of deal and loan packages has he negotiated with that bank?"

"I don't know exactly, but I can find out, and then I am going to try to negotiate a better deal."

"Fine."

A week or so later, we were back talking on the phone. "Phyllis, how did it go?"

"How did what go?" she responded.

"You know, how did it go with negotiating with Lambert Builders?"

"Bill Lambert won't even negotiate with us."

"Why?" I asked.

"Don't know."

"Well, let's look at this. Why don't you see if you can

You have to exceed the other person's BOON to get from No to Go.

NO ONE IS GOING TO TAKE LESS FROM YOU THAN WHAT THEY CAN GET FROM THEIR BOON.

offer him a better deal than the bank he is currently doing business with? If so, then we can work out something, I'm sure."

"Fine, I will check it and give you a call."

A few days later, this is the conversation that took place.

"Rob, I checked out what we could offer Lambert Construction, and we can't beat the deal he has with National Bank."

"That is it, then, Phyllis."

"No, Rob, we still want his business."

"What do you mean, you still want his business?"

"Yes, we want to negotiate with him and get his new construction business, as he is expanding north of the city, and we feel his business is the kind we want more of."

I said, "Phyllis, let's go over something to be sure we are communicating. Are you saying that you are trying to get Lambert to come into your bank and do business with you guys when you either can't or won't offer him as good a deal as he has now, and preferably a better one?"

"Well, if you put it that way, yes."

"Think about it: No one is going to negotiate a deal with you that is worse than their BOON, their Best Option Outside Negotiation. Until you can either meet or, better yet, exceed Lambert's BOON, there will be no deal."

No one in any negotiation is going to give you a better deal than they can get somewhere else and that somewhere is their BOON. The BOON is where you walk to when you don't get agreement with the party you are negotiating with. That might be to do nothing. It might be to purchase the item from someone else, to go to another job offer, to wait for the next deal to come along.

So, knowing the other person's BOON tells you what you are going to have to beat in order to make the deal with that party. It will set the limits of the agreement and govern much of the give-and-take of the negotiation.

If I perceive my BOON to be X, I am not going to settle with you for anything less than X, and certainly I will strive to get something more than X from you.

Perception is always important, and certainly it is here. What happens if the other party thinks their BOON is better than it really is? They will be harder to negotiate with because they will think they are stronger than they really are. They think their BOON is stronger than it really is.

The above scenario is neither good for you nor for them. It is not a kind, loving, creative, caring, bright, winning act on your part to allow the other party to walk away from a negotiation with you to a lesser BOON than you can give them. They will lose when they discover their best option was not as good as what they could have gotten from you, and you will lose for not having been able to put together the deal. No good for either party.

When you know their BOON and you know that it is not as good as you are willing to give them, you need to educate them. "You know, Harold, we really should be able to put this deal together. My sense of it, and I may be wrong, is that you feel you have a better deal waiting for you than I can offer you. Is that correct? If so, do you mind telling me where you are going to go if we don't put the deal together and give us at least a chance to match your BOON?"

They may well say something like "Well, Rob, you've got to at least meet and exceed our deal that we can strike with STX Corporation, which is …" This now gives you some sense of where and what they see as their BOON or alternative to making a deal with you is.

Note: If you can't at least meet and/or better the other party's perceived BOON, you have no deal with them. No, repeat, no one is going to give you more or take less from you than what they think they can get

PERCEPTION CAN BE MORE IMPORTANT THAN REALITY.

outside with someone else. So you'd better have as good an idea as possible of what the other party's BOON really is. Then you have to be willing and able to match or exceed it to get the deal done.

> *One must not tie a ship to a single anchor, nor life to a single hope.*
> —Epictetus

30

Don't Make the Deal So Good That It Is Bad

Even when you can do so, taking everything off the table may not be the best thing. The concessions that you purposely leave on the negotiating table may be vital to crafting a winning agreement. There is nothing written in stone by the Wisdom of Great Negotiators that says you have to strike the hardest deal, extracting the very last possible concession from your counterpart. In fact, a lot of hard data indicate that doing so may be one of the worst things you can do. You have made the deal so good (for you, at least at first glance) that it's actually bad negotiating, as the deal will not be lived up to.

There's a fine line between crafting the best deal possible and being too greedy. Greed is one of the cardinal sins of life and can very much work against wise, successful negotiating.

When you extract that last remaining concession from your counterpart, when you drive that last nail into the contract, when you leave the other party feeling destitute and taken advantage of, then watch out. Concessions gained and victories thought won may be extremely short-lived. You may find you negotiated a false victory that is coming back to haunt you in ways never dreamed of.

For example, it may seem like a good idea at the time to:

> **There's a fine line between making the best deal possible and being greedy.**

POWER CAN CORRUPT. USE IT WISELY.

➤ Require your distributor to open additional field offices to serve your firm, even though they can't afford the additional overhead and justify the cost for value received.

➤ Require your supplier to inventory goods for twice the normal time period.

➤ Ask for 120 days' credit instead of the normal 30 days.

➤ Write into the contract heavy penalty clauses for minor nonperformance issues.

➤ Demand an exclusivity arrangement with your vendors to their detriment.

All of us can add to this list almost indefinitely, especially when we are negotiating from a position of strength and power. Power can be intoxicating and can corrupt what might otherwise have been a good person or a good negotiation. Baron Acton said, "Power tends to corrupt and absolute power corrupts absolutely."

Admonition: The stronger you are in a negotiation, the more attention you should pay to how you are crafting the "hard" agreements, the ones that are given only because you are in a position to demand them of the other party.

Simply because you are the largest or most important client of your negotiating counterpart doesn't necessarily mean it is in your best interest to knock down their profit margin to the extent that their backs are against the wall. You can do so, but is it in your own best interest—let alone theirs?

> *There are occasions when it is undoubtedly better to incur loss than to make a gain.*
> —Titus Maccius Plautus

31

YOU DO WHAT YOU CAN DO

STRIVING TO GAIN what you want from others and in the process giving them what they want from you is one of life's most challenging adventures. There are times when, in trying to get from No to Go, you face overwhelming odds. A negotiation situation may seem out of your control. You may lack resources with which to conduct the transaction. The other party may be overwhelming in their demands, intractable in their positions, hardnosed in their dealings with you. It's tough, but you are still in the game—you do what you can do to get from them what you want.

Doing what you can do will involve forbearance, tolerance, strong will, and fortitude to act against what seem like overwhelming odds. Like the little bird in the following story, "you do what you can do."

> **SOMETIMES WE SIMPLY HAVE TO DO WHAT WE CAN DO—AND LIVE WITH IT.**

One Stormy Evening

One stormy evening, a farmer was returning home on horseback when he noticed a little bird in a furrow in the field. The little bird was lying on his back with his little spindly feet sticking straight up toward the sky.

"What are you doing, little birdie?" asked the farmer. "I heard the sky was going to fall," replied the bird.

"Well, holding your little feet up to the sky won't help," said the farmer. The birdie replied, "Well, you do what you can do."

Haven't we all at some time in our life felt like that little bird, struggling against overwhelming odds? An effort to gain an agreement that seemed as illusive as it was difficult. A time when everything seemed to be going wrong. Your timing was off; the other party had information you didn't and couldn't obtain that worked against you. Your team partner alienated the other party to the point they were ready to call it quits, which would have meant major damage to you and your organization.

It was a worst nightmare. Nothing worse could happen. What do you do? Like that little birdie in the story, we simply bite the bullet and do what we can do, no more and certainly no less.

What do you do when all seems to be going from bad to worse?

➤ Call time-out.

➤ Visualize the worst-case scenario and ask yourself whether you can live with that.

- Call for help.
- Reassess the situation and look for deficiencies in the other party's position.
- Be clear about what you have that they want and how you plan to get it.
- Assess your power sources.
- Check what your perspective is.
- Be alert—watch your state of mind.

> **THERE ARE TIMES WHEN WE MUST "DO WHAT WE CAN DO" AND LEAVE IT AT THAT.**

This little birdie could have played the role of victim and moaned that there was nothing he could do. He did what he could do.

He didn't ask, "Hey, is this going to work?" He didn't do a cost/benefit analysis of the situation, or at least not that he brought forth. He didn't call in consultants. He basically looked at the situation from his vantage point and did what he felt he could do, which was to raise his spindly legs up to the darkened heavens above.

None of us is going to find ourselves in such a helpless situation in our negotiations as the little bird found himself in, out there in the muddy field that late wintry afternoon.

There will be times, though, when we will have to simply "do what we can do" and leave it at that.

I have known many who could not when they could for they had not done it when they could.
—François Rabelais

Section V

The Give-and-Take to Get to Go

32. "Hollywooding" your concessions.

33. Have a strong rationale for your demands.

34. Never make a negotiating concession without making it conditional.

35. Never accept the first offer—you will never be forgiven

36. Guard against splitting the difference.

37. Don't concede until you know all the demands that relate to that concession.

38. Don't honor an out-of-place or low demand.

39. Give concessions that are of high value to the other party and which cost you little.

32

"HOLLYWOODING" YOUR CONCESSIONS

MR. AND MRS. ANDERSON were in their early eighties when they decided to sell their home and move to a smaller condominium in a nearby retirement center. They had listed the home for $300,000. A young couple had made an offer, and the parties were about 10 percent, or about $30,000, apart, as I understand it. Well, that isn't much more than the standard 6 or 7 percent real estate commission, so it should not have posed any insurmountable barriers to the sale and negotiation of the home.

One Sunday after church, I was over visiting with Mr. Anderson when the young couple came with their broker to see the house again. Mr. Anderson greeted them and said, "Welcome. You know, Mrs. Anderson and I were just talking about you youngsters last night, and we believe that we are going to be able to put this transaction together, and you and your young family are going to be able to live in this lovely home."

"Well, we think so, too, Mr. Anderson," the couple responded.

The real estate broker, of course, nodded his agreement. (He had probably already mentally spent the hoped-for commission.)

Mr. Anderson then said, "Based on that assumption, come with me for a minute." We all followed him out through the large backyard to an extended double garage. Into the garage we went, and there in front of us was a

DON'T UNDER-ESTIMATE THE POWER OF PACKAGING YOUR CONCESSIONS.

LESSON 1

"HOLLYWOOD-ING" PUTS VALUE ON THE CONCESSION GIVEN.

little sailboat. Now, I don't know much about sailboats, but I would guess that it needed some paint and probably a new sail. How much was it worth? Perhaps $1,000 or $1,500 at the most?

Mr. Anderson said to the young couple, "You know, Mrs. Anderson and I talked about this last night, and based on the premise that you folks are going to be able to purchase this home for your lovely family, we want to give you this sailboat with no strings attached."

When I heard "with no strings attached," red lights went on in my mind. Bells went off, ding, ding! It was sort of an "I am from the IRS and am here to help you" kind of nonsense.

Then Mr. Anderson went on to say, "If you young folks have half as much joy and celebration in this boat with your young children as we have had with our grandchildren sailing in this boat, your lives will be enriched beyond all measure. We would take this very sailboat you see in front of you down to the Colorado lakes just before sunset. And as we were putting the boat into the lake, the winds of the west would invariably come up, moving us out into the middle of the lake, in family unity."

As I was listening to Mr. Anderson talk, I thought to myself, "If these kids don't buy this home, I, Rob Rutherford, am going to buy that boat." And I hate boats! I get seasick just looking at pictures of boats in magazines.

Anderson had just "Hollywooded" his concession, making it dramatic, putting life into it, giving it added value, being excited about it. I personally thought he overdid it when he said to the couple, "Get into the boat." In any event, some weeks later the couple in fact did buy the home. Now, I don't know how much they paid for the home; it is not my business, and I really don't care. But I can almost assure you that that little beat-up boat Mr. Anderson gave that young couple with no

124   FROM NO TO GO

strings attached probably cost them at least $20,000 in terms of what they paid extra for the house over their first offer. Now, I could be wrong, but I seldom am in these situations.

That is what I mean by "Hollywooding" your concession.

Now Anderson could have said to the couple, "Look, here is this dilapidated junker of what is left of a sailboat. If you don't take it off our hands, my wife and I have decided to chop it up for kindling wood." Frankly, that would probably have been closer to the true value of the boat.

How you give a concession is often more important than *what* you give as a concession. When you fail to put value on a concession you give, you can be assured the recipient of the concession will put less value on it likewise.

I have great respect for Hollywood, as I grew up there and graduated from Hollywood High School. So Hollywooding—if there is such a word—is a way of adding respect and excitement, of packaging, merchandising if you will, that is so important in sales and negotiating and life.

Think about it for a minute. What is Kentucky Fried Chicken? Is it delicious, twenty-one herbs and spices, finger-licking good Kentucky Fried Chicken, or simply fried dead chicken? Well, how many people would buy KFC if it were packaged and advertised as "Come into your local KFC and get some fried dead chicken"?

When you are making a list of possible gives (concessions) you have or are willing to exchange for what you want to get from the other party, think of Hollywooding one or two of them. At a minimum, think how you might put added value on them, make them shine more brightly in the eyes of the other party. It can pay big dividends to you, and the other party will appreciate and value more what you have given them. They will feel they got more from you, and that will make them feel better about the negotiation. Recall that the one thing we know about nego-

A LITTLE "HOLLYWOODING" PAYS BIG DIVIDENDS.

tiating is that the other party wants to feel good about having negotiated with you. What easier and better way is there than to pay some attention to how you give your concession? Hollywooding is one inexpensive, smart way to help the other party feel good. You will get excited and feel good about the concession as well.

> *It isn't what I do, but how I do it.*
> *It isn't what I say, but how I say it.*
> *And how I look when I do and say it.*
> —Mae West

33

HAVE A STRONG RATIONALE FOR YOUR DEMANDS

ALL SUCCESSFUL negotiators know how to make strong, believable, and ultimately acceptable demands in their dealings with others.

One of the easiest and simplest ways to increase your negotiating power is to provide each of your demands with strong rationales. The rationale is the reason why the other party should give you what you just asked for.

You are in a business discussion with a vendor. You say to your counterpart, "Fred, we have to have a 10 percent price reduction on that line item." Now that is the demand: a 10 percent price reduction.

The rationale might be:

➤ We are going to give you twice the normal order.

➤ We will pay you all cash.

➤ If you don't give it to us, we will be forced to go to your competition.

➤ It is standard in the business.

➤ That is what we have always gotten from you during all the time we have done business together.

➤ By accommodating us on this now, we can expect to do much business in the future.

THE RATIONALE IS THE REASON WHY THEY (THE OTHER PARTY) SHOULD GIVE YOU WHAT YOU ASKED FOR.

THE STRONGER THE RATIONALE, THE STRONGER THE DEMANDS.

Clearly the other party may not give you what you want, but they will have to deal not only with the demand (that is, the 10 percent price reduction on that line item) but also with the rationale (the right to make this demand on them in the first place), and even defeat or destroy that rationale.

The next time someone makes a demand on you in a negotiation, study their rationale. Say, "Fred, what is your rationale for asking for a 10 percent price reduction?"

Fred will want to be very sure that whatever rationale he gives to defend his right to make this demand (and for the other party to give Fred what Fred asked for), he can defend it and make it at least partially believable. There is a direct corollary between the demand and the rationale. The stronger the demand, the stronger the rationale; the weaker the demand, the weaker the rationale as perceived by the negotiating parties.

If your demands are not being given serious consideration and are not being met, chances are really good that the rationales are not compelling to the other party. Why?

- ➤ It may be because your interests and those of the other party are not compatible, and the deal is not meant to be.

- ➤ Assuming you have comparable interests, then the other party cannot see the value and benefit in what you have presented. It's up to you to show them how they benefit and how that benefit warrants entering into an agreement.

- ➤ You assume they know what the benefits are to them, but they don't know.

- ➤ You haven't spelled out the benefits clearly enough so that the other party can truly see that justification in what you are asking from them.

"Great, Rob," you might say, "but I can't think of any rationale other than that is what I want." I guess you could go with that as a last resort, but it probably won't be terribly motivating to the other party. "Fred, you will have to give me a 10 percent price reduction on that line item, simply because I want it."

A savvy counterpart might ask you why you want it. "Because," you say, "it will help keep me in business, and I can do business with you year after year." Or, "Because if I don't get the 10 percent price reduction, I will have to go to another source, and I don't want to do that." All of these, of course, are rationales, and they might be good ones at that in this situation.

If you cannot think of a good rationale, chances are pretty good that:

➤ You don't have a good justification for making your demand in the first place.

➤ Your demand will be seen as weak and treated as such by the other party.

➤ You will have little or no chance of getting what you are asking for.

➤ Your demand doesn't merit being given serious consideration.

If any or all of these statements are so in your case, you had better either give up that specific demand or go back and develop one or more strong rationales for what you want.

Take each demand and develop the strongest rationale possible. If you find you cannot think of any good rationale, it is safe to say that your demand is going to be weak and even insupportable. You need to either go out and develop stronger justifications for your demands or change your demands until you can support them.

COMPELLING RATIONALES MAKE COMPELLING DEMANDS.

IF YOUR RATIONALE CAN'T STAND UP UNDER ATTACK, YOUR DEMANDS WILL NOT STAND UP EITHER.

Compelling rationales make compelling demands that maximize your chances of getting what you are asking for. What are some reasons why the other party might feel your demands are justifiable?

➤ They want your business.

➤ They like you.

➤ Your offer is fair from their point of view.

➤ They don't want you to take your business somewhere else.

➤ It is better than their Best Option Outside Negotiation (BOON).

Know the other party and what they value from you. Construct your rationale to correspond with that value. By doing so, you greatly enhance the chance of your offer being accepted.

"Fred, both of our firms want to do business together, is that correct?"

"Right."

"Okay. In order for us to give you the kind of support you need, and the kind that we take pride in delivering, we are going to have to gain an exclusive agreement from you for at least the first two years. Even that is not going to be enough time to recoup our original investment in you. We are confident, though, that after you see what we can do for you, we will continue on long after the original two-year agreement is over.

"Additionally, by both our firms' entering into this two-year agreement, we are assured that both parties will be committed to its success. It makes it a real two-way, mutually advantageous street for our respective firms to travel on."

If the rationale is the reason why they should give you what you asked for, then it follows that if the other party can destroy your rationale, they can destroy your demand. By attacking your rationale, they attack your demand. If your rationale can't stand up under fire, your demands certainly will not stand up either.

Perception is critical here. If your rationale is not perceived to be legitimate or strong in the eyes of the other party, it isn't strong, even if it is in reality. The other party must see the worth of the rationale. Sometimes in negotiating, you might have to take time to educate the other party, to thoroughly go over with them what the rationale is and why you have the right to ask for what you just did.

Let's take the example just used: "We have to have a 10 percent price reduction on that line item." That is the demand. The rationale might be "in order to give you twice the normal order." Now that is a benefit to the other party; assuming that they want twice the order, it is a positive benefit. You are in control whether or not you will give twice the order.

In another example: "We have to have a 10 percent price reduction on that line item, or we will have to take our business somewhere else." Now that is a negative benefit, assuming that they want your business. ("Negative benefit" might sound like an oxymoron.)

Let's say you are in control of taking your business somewhere else, so the two tests—the rationale must be of benefit to the other party, and you must be in control—are met.

We are not saying that because your demand has a strong rationale it will be accepted by the other party. But assuredly, if your demands don't have strong rationales, they will not be met.

You need to be in control because if the other party doesn't want to give you what you asked for (and often they don't, right?), they can destroy your demand by destroying your rationale. So stay in control.

IF THEY DESTROY YOUR RATIONALE, THEY DESTROY YOUR DEMAND.

HAVE A STRONG RATIONALE

Example: "We have to have a 10 percent price reduction on that line item because it won't affect your bottom line or your cash flow at all."

Hold it. Unless we are privy to their books, which we are not, we are not in control of that rationale. If they say, "The heck it won't; it will adversely affect our bottom line and cash flow," what have they done to your demand? Destroyed it. So don't let them pull the rug out from underneath you—stay in control of your rationale.

All successful negotiators understand the art of making strong demands. They back up their demands by strong rationales that are in benefit terms to the other party, and the successful negotiator stays in control of the demand and doesn't let anyone "pull the rug out from underneath them."

They follow very closely the principles just outlined in this lesson on how to "have a strong rationale for your demands." They know it works.

> *You never know what is enough unless you know what is more than enough.*
> —William Blake

34

NEVER MAKE A NEGOTIATING CONCESSION WITHOUT MAKING IT CONDITIONAL

I KNOW THAT YOU should never say never ... but in negotiating there is a cardinal rule that says you should never give up something unless you get something back in return. Now, what you get back does not necessarily have to be equal. In fact, it seldom is.

You don't even have to know what you want in return. You might simply say, "If I were to give you a price reduction on that line item, what would you be able to give me back in return?" Then wait to see what that person would give for your concession. It's possible they would offer to give you something that was more valuable than what you might have thought of asking for. It is also possible that you have not thought of asking for what they offered. What they offered might cost little or nothing, yet be of substantial value to you.

In lieu of asking for something specific in return, the other party might godfather their concession. Do you remember the scene in the movie *The Godfather* when the Godfather has just saved a young guy from some horrible situation? And the young man is so thankful and says, "Godfather, what can I possibly do for you in return?"

THE ONLY REASON YOU WOULD GIVE A CONCESSION IS TO GET SOMETHING BACK IN RETURN.

CONDITIONAL CONCESSIONS

BE LEERY OF SOMEONE GODFATHER-ING THEIR CONCESSION TO YOU.

And the Godfather pauses a moment and says, "Son, there will come a time when I will call on you."

Wow! I don't know about you, but I certainly do not want anyone godfathering me! I want to know what the other party wants in return for what they have done for me. In other words, what is their concession going to cost me?

The important reason for making a concession conditional is that this is what negotiating is all about: a give-and-take process.

Now you might say, "Well, Rob, it doesn't make all that much difference, does it, really? Can't I—just because I want to be seen as a good guy—give up something without making it conditional on getting something back in return?"

My response to that is NO. That is, unless you don't mind being taken advantage of, being seen as an easy hit, not knowing what you are doing.

If you don't make your concession conditional, the other party will think you're an easy hit and smell blood. Now that may strike you as overstating the case—never making a concession in the negotiating arena without making it conditional. You be the judge.

Let's take an example. Say of one your kids wants to take out the family car Friday evening. He says to you, "Dad, I would like to borrow the car tonight. Is that okay?"

Now what do you say? Depends, doesn't it? It depends on whether you are negotiating with your kid. If you are, then you don't let him have the car without making it conditional on getting something back in return. So you say something like "Well, son, I was thinking of taking it out tonight with your mom, but okay, you can have it if you check the right front tire—it seems low on air—and put $10 worth of gas in the car so you can go at least fifteen miles."

So there you have it. You have negotiated with your son for the car.

Now you might be thinking, *Wait a minute, Rob. After all, I am his dad!*

Okay, so are you negotiating or not? If you are, you now know *you have to make any concession conditional.* You say, "Well, all I want him to do is to think I am a pretty neat dad for loaning him the car tonight." Great—then that is the condition, that your son thinks you are a neat dad.

Better check that out, though. You say to him, "Son, if I let you use the family car tonight, will you think your dad is a pretty neat guy?" Then wait for the answer. If he says to you, "Sure, Dad," then you are a neat guy—and the condition has been met. But if he says, "No, Dad, you are still a real jerk," then the kid walks or, at a minimum, drives someone else's car, not yours. Why? Because he has failed to met the negotiating rule, which is *Never make a concession without making it conditional.*

BE SURE THAT YOU KNOW IF YOU ARE NEGOTIATING OR NOT.

> *Only when an individual gives up something he has in an exchange can you know how much he values the thing he says he desires.*
> —Harry Browne

35

NEVER ACCEPT THE FIRST OFFER— YOU WILL NEVER BE FORGIVEN

WHEN I WAS a college professor, I had a growing family and needed a larger home, but first had to sell the smaller one we were living in. I was not very knowledgeable at that time about real estate. The broker handling the marketing of my house suggested we put the price of the home higher than what it was expected to sell for, thus giving some selling negotiating room. I listed the house for $40,000 (so you know how long ago that must have been in California), expecting to get maybe $35,000 if fortunate. We might have to take $33,000 if the market didn't respond because I had already made what for me was a substantial deposit to buy the larger house.

The broker explained that in about a week, I could expect a lot of interest in the home when all the other brokers' offices had received a copy of the listing. Until then I would have to be patient. The next day, I got a call from the broker saying he had an offer on the house and wanted to go over it with me. He did, and it was a full-price, full-term offer meeting all my listing requirements. To the best of my recollection, there wasn't even a weasel clause in it, such as being subject to final in-

> **IF YOU WANT TO UPSET SOMEONE IN A NEGOTIATION, ACCEPT HIS OR HER FIRST OFFER.**

spectation and approval of the Conditions, Covenants, and Restrictions (CCRs), or subject to obtaining available financing or anything else.

I couldn't believe it. My first offer to sell my house was accepted without any conditions or reservations. It hadn't even been listed for twenty-four hours. To the best of my knowledge, no one except my broker had even known the house was on the market, let alone seen it. And now I had a full-price-term offer to buy.

How do you think I felt? I was upset. I wanted to know what the buyer knew about my home that I didn't know. Was it sitting on some kind of mineral rights? Was there some secret commercial development plan afoot that would make my home far more valuable than before? Was there something special about the home that was unknown to me and known to the buyer?

I didn't want to sell. The broker saw that I was upset. He said, "Rob, you are upset."

I said, "Yes, I am, because maybe the house is worth more than $40,000. Here the first person and the only person who saw it made me a full-price offer with no conditions placed on it. I don't want to sell the house at that price."

The broker said, "No problem, you don't have to sell your house at any price if you don't want to."

"I don't?" I said. "But I signed a contract to sell my house."

"No," the broker kindly said. "You didn't sign a contract to sell the house, but you did sign a listing contract that agrees to pay me a 6 percent commission if I find a ready, willing, and able buyer who meets all your conditions for the sale of the house, which this offer does. So, Rob, you don't have to sell the house to the buyer, but you do have to pay me a full 6 percent commission."

It was at that moment that I believe I got a revelation. If this broker could make a living selling real estate like this and treating his clients as he did, I could make

You got your asking price, so why is there a problem?

Never Accept First Offer

137

Is it better to give someone less and have them feel good, or give them more and have them feel bad?

a small fortune if I went into the real estate business. And wherever he might be, I thank him, for that is exactly what I did. I went into the real estate business, and fortune and fate were very kind to me and my family.

You might be wondering whether I sold the house to this potential buyer. Yes, I did. I sold the house to him.

Let's look at some negotiation principles here. First, the buyer violated the principle of never accepting the first offer because you will never be forgiven. And I was unforgiving toward him. I wondered what the true value of the house might be. Maybe it was worth $45,000 or $50,000. I would never really know. I was upset.

Now you might say, "Well, Rob, you got your asking price and that was better than you had expected, so you should have been more than happy with the sale." Yes, I know. Thank you for telling me that. But there are a lot of "should haves" in all of our worlds.

I would like to relate something that happened a few weeks later when I was turning over the keys and explaining some of the features of the house to the new owner. As selling the house on the first offer was still weighing heavily on my mind, I asked him point-blank why he bought the house and didn't attempt to negotiate any of its price or terms. What he said was, "I feel I paid too much for the house. I don't think it was worth $40,000. I don't, quite frankly, think it was worth $35,000, but I didn't feel I was in any position to negotiate, let alone bargain or dicker around with the price and terms. A few months ago I transferred here from Chicago to work for Ratheon. My wife and three school-age children are still in Chicago. Now it's getting late in the summer, school is to begin in a few weeks, and we still had not found a house to our liking. We like this area very much, but no homes were for sale. When your home came on the market, I didn't want to take any chance of not getting it. My wife had informed me a few days before that if I didn't find the family a house within the next two weeks, she and the three children would not be moving out to Santa Barbara until the next year after school was out in Chicago. So you see, I was under duress and pressure to buy a house NOW, and yours was it."

Now, when I heard his story, how do you think I felt now about selling my house on the first full-price offer? Better, but now another thought came up. What would I have done about selling the house if I had known about the buyer's situation that he just described to me? Would I have done anything differently? I know some of you are probably saying, "Yes, Rob, if you had known of his predicament and the pressure and time deadlines he was facing, you would have upped the price." Oh, how can you think such awful thoughts? So, "never accept the first offer; you will never be forgiven."

How do you think the buyer would have felt if I had said, "Well, Harold, I certainly would have sold the house for $35,000 and maybe even less if it had been on the market a little longer. You overpaid for the house." Now how would Harold have felt? Would he have felt differently if I had said, "You know, Harold, while you might not be sure the house is worth $40,000, there were some market indicators after you bought the house that were showing that it was a very fair price and maybe even too low. Past sales are exactly that—indicators of past worth. The market, I understand, is improving rapidly, there are few if any houses of this kind on the market, and you got a really good buy. Our loss is your gain"? Or at least something like that. Why not make Harold's day and give Harold some bragging rights that he can take

IT COSTS LITTLE TO LET THE OTHER PARTY KNOW THAT THEY GOT A GOOD DEAL.

back home to Chicago as he readies his family to move out to the West Coast?

Remember: The one thing we know about negotiating is that the other party wants to feel good about negotiating with you. Does it really cost anything to let the other party know that they have a good deal, as in the example in this lesson? It is sad that some people never learn how to give graciously and how to get graciously.

> *Many men go fishing all their lives without knowing it is not the fish they are after.*
> —Henry David Thoreau

36

Guard against splitting the difference

"Let's be fair and split the difference" is probably heard more times in moving to end a negotiation than any other phrase. "Let's be fair and split the difference" is seldom the best solution to gaining an agreement, and is almost never the most creative. Splitting the difference often obscures the opportunity to create more value for each party. It is the lazy way out. It may be expeditious at times and acceptable to both parties, but it generally leaves at least one party getting less than they had wanted. Furthermore, if the parties know that splitting the difference is apt to be offered as the way to settle, then starting positions are set higher than can be defended. Energy is devoted to concessions here and there, game-playing that hinders the creative, mutual, problem-solving process that could very often lead to greater value and gains for both parties.

A wonderful example of a creative alternative to splitting the difference is shown in this story of two sisters who wanted the same orange. Now, conventional wisdom would say, "Okay, one of you gets to cut the orange in half and the other gets to choose which half she wants." (This approach is not limited to oranges. How about pies, cakes, and other good things?) But before this split-the-difference solution to sharing the one orange,

By splitting the difference, you often lose the opportunity to create more value for each party.

Splitting the Difference 141

one sister, Susan, luckily asked her sister, Ann, "What do you want the orange for?" Good question. "I want to make orange juice," Ann responded. "Good," Susan said, "then you can give me the orange peelings, as I want to grind them up to add to the spices of a cake I am going to bake."

One orange. The two parties had two entirely different wants from the same orange, giving them the opportunity to meet each other's goals in a far better way than the traditional "splitting the difference."

In purchasing a home, a car, or a refrigerator, price is only one item. There are delivery charges, warranties, terms, and add-on values that are negotiable. Instead of splitting the difference on price, one party might want better terms, whereas to the other party, price is more important.

Negotiating parties have different needs, views, perspectives, wants, and purposes, which is why negotiating is such a powerful, learnable life tool.

> *When ideas fail, words come in very handy.*
> —Goethe

37

Don't concede until you know all the demands that relate to that concession

On a Friday evening one fall, my eighteen-year-old son, a senior in high school at the time, asked, "Dad, can I have the family van [more like a bus than a van] tonight?"

"Well, kid, I was thinking about taking it out myself this evening, but if you will put at least $10 of gas in the car so it can go at least fifteen miles tonight [it was hard on gasoline] and check the left front tire, which looks low on air, fine. Take it."

Let's pause a moment here to analyze the beginning of this event. Was I negotiating with my eighteen-year-old son? Yes. What was the exchange? The use of the car that evening for at least $10 worth of gas and a tire check. Okay. So far so good. Because we are negotiating, conditions had to be put on the concessions made. Okay.

Now suppose my son had then said, "Oh, by the way, Dad, I won't have the van back home tonight by midnight, as is our regular family policy. In fact, Dad, I won't have the van home until probably around 3:30 or 4:00 A.M., as

Check to see if there are additional demands before making the concession.

Wait Before Conceding   143

we are going down to the Arvada High School basketball game tonight. And by the way, Dad, there will be more than three unrelated kids in the van tonight. As a matter of fact, there will be our whole offensive Fairview High School football team in the car, and by the way, Dad, you know that large space in the back of the van? Well, we are going to have a keg of beer back there, Dad, but that's okay, as we have hired Riley to drive. You know Riley, don't you, Dad? He is a Mormon and doesn't drink, so he is designated driver tonight. And by the way, Dad …"

WAIT—WAIT A MINUTE! After hearing the additional demands for concessions—bringing car home late, thirteen kids in the van, beer—you very well might not want to make the first concession and conditions you made now that you know what the additional demands are to be.

While negotiating, if you feel the other party may make additional demands on you after you have made what you believed to be the final concession to get the agreement, ask about it. "Fred, by making this concession, does that close the deal?" Or, "Fred, before I respond to your request for additional time to put the transaction together, are there any other requests you have relative to this project?" You might also say, "Fine, Fred, and if there are further demands, we can renegotiate the whole agreement."

Making additional demands (or requests or adding further requirements) is often a ploy on the part of the other party to get you to concede more than you originally thought you were, at no expense to them and at a cost to you.

Stand ready to take back what you have given out if the circumstances have changed against you in a negative way. A deal isn't a deal until it is over and done with.

*Even if you're on the right track,
you'll get run over if you just sit there.*
—Will Rogers

38

Don't honor an out-of-place high or low demand

The Sorenson Company, a small manufacturing firm, was in a civil legal dispute with the federal government over some alleged environmental infractions. The federal government representatives made an incredibly high monetary demand, using a government formula that figured in alleged loss to the government, penalties multiplied, and back interest accrued.

First, there was no way that the Sorenson firm could even consider the demands. They would have been forced to file for bankruptcy. The demands were so far out of line and lacking in justification that Sorenson chose not to honor them.

Yet Sorenson was in a dilemma because he faced mounting legal costs to defend the company's position against government charges and demands. Sorenson, at the same time, refused to negotiate with the government as long as it was making these outlandish monetary demands on his company.

After much perseverance and intense legal maneuvering and strategy, a negotiated agreement was reached. The final figures were a fraction of the government's original demand on the Sorenson Company.

Be ready to take back what you have given if the situation changes against you.

It is doubtful that the government ever thought it would come anywhere close to the original amount demanded. The reasoning may have been to make an outlandish demand and then settle for substantially less, but far more than Sorenson would have felt was reasonable.

The government's demand was meant to scare, to intimidate, and to present a hardnosed, at first intractable negotiating position to gain the upper hand against Sorenson. The purpose of doing this more than likely was to lower Sorenson's expectations of what the final dollar outcome would be.

By not honoring the government's out-of-place high demand, Sorenson avoided falling into the trap of trying to appease their adversary—in this case by throwing money at them in the hopes of getting them to go away.

The final settlement was a fraction of the original monetary demand. Who negotiated well? Who won and lost? Who got the best deal out of a very adversarial and legalistic encounter? That is up to personal interpretation.

In your negotiation with vendors, government officials, customers, competitors, sellers, and buyers, any one of these parties might make an off-the-wall demand of you. They are hoping to intimidate you, to throw you off balance, to get you to make a counteroffer so much higher than you ever wanted it to be in the first place.

In the dog-eat-dog world of competition, the off-the-wall demand maker may figure it's each person for himself. Maybe, they think, you might be just dumb enough to give in to such outrageous demands.

More likely the demanding party is trying to intimidate and scare you. One of the continual principles of master negotiating in life is: Don't let them scare you! Don't let them intimidate you. What happens on the outside of your life in negotiating, you may not be able to control. But what you do with that outside happening within your mind, you do have much control over.

HIGH DEMANDS ARE OFTEN DESIGNED TO INTIMIDATE YOU.

OUT-OF-PLACE DEMANDS

Guard against unreasonable demands by knowing your negotiating strengths and limitations.

The out-of-place high demand is also designed to get you to overrespond to the demand and to come back with a counteroffer that is far more than you ever intended to pay or give on final settlement, let alone on the first response.

Suppose they are demanding $20,000 to sign off on the project, and you were expecting at most to pay $3,500, depending on various conditions and release clauses. If you honor their demand by counteroffering, you have given their offer legitimacy. The counteroffer more than likely is going to be higher than you ever intended. Your counteroffer, to be credible in light of the high demand from the other party, puts you higher and higher than you ever wanted or expected to be.

In this example, how can you counteroffer at $3,000 if they are demanding $20,000? The other party is trying to intimidate you into making a higher counteroffer than you would ever have made, barring their high outlandish demand.

So you violate "the don't honor an out-of-place high demand" principle, and you offer $4,000, much higher than you ever wanted to go. They then magnanimously compromise and offer to sign off on the project for $15,000. You offer $5,000, and in a seeming spirit of resignation and an attitude of "after all the time and effort we have spent," they offer, under all these circumstances, to "be fair and split the difference." Wait. "Let's be fair and split the difference" between $5,000 and their $15,000 would be $10,000. At $5,000 you are much higher than you ever intended to be, and now the other party's calling on you to be fair and split the difference, making the deal close at $10,000.

Don't honor that, or else you will be sucked into overpaying, even at the "let's be fair and split the difference" proposal and ploy.

They are also attempting to set the stage to be seen as the great compromiser and you as the uncooperative person who is an obstacle to agreement.

One of the most effective ways to confront outlandish, unreasonable, unacceptable demands is to know and adhere to your negotiating strengths and limitations. Know what you want and how strong your position is; know and adhere to your negotiation limits—limits you will not go beyond. In general, the limits you have established are based largely on what you have lined up outside this agreement. In other words, where do you go, where do you walk to, if you don't get an agreement with this particular party?

It is possible in rare cases that the out-of-place high demand is simply made by one who has no clue as to the actual reality of what they are negotiating about. With luck, you can put on your teacher's hat and educate them on the reality of the negotiating situation, and doing so will solve the out-of-place high demand obstacle.

The attitude of the out-of-place high demand maker is that if you are dumb enough or gullible enough to react to it and counteroffer, that is your problem, not theirs.

Making ridiculous high (or low) demands has its own built-in potential risks. One is that the unreasonably high demands or the low-ball offer will so alienate the other party as to exclude any chance of gaining a viable negotiated agreement. They will refuse to do business with you, even when you have decided to make them a reasonable offer that they would most certainly take. Your unreasonable offer has offended them, and they will make their deal with someone else—someone who honors their intelligence more, who is more reasonable and worth more, at least in their eyes.

The Brownings put their home on the market at a reasonable price. Immediately they received a low-ball

DON'T ALLOW THE OTHER PARTY TO FEEL YOU ARE GETTING TOO GOOD A DEAL FROM THEM.

Leaving the door ajar gives the possibility of renegotiating at a later time.

offer from the Myers. The Brownings felt it was purposely low, designed to get them to lower their already fair price to some ridiculous price. The Brownings refused to honor the low, out-of-place demand or offer. They wouldn't counteroffer.

Then the Myers made another offer, close enough to the asking price that it seemed highly likely that the sale could be negotiated. The Brownings refused to negotiate with the Myers, even when the Myers later offered them more for their home than they were asking. Too late. The damage, at least in the eyes of the Brownings, had already been irrevocably done.

The Brownings, interestingly enough, sold their home shortly afterwards to a young couple they liked at a price substantially lower than what the Myers had eventually offered them.

Why? In part because they were angry at the Myers' offer. Also, they liked the young couple. Perhaps the couple reminded the Brownings of themselves when they were that age. Who knows for sure? What we do know for sure is that the human aspect of negotiating can be just as important as and often more important than all the other elements—price, delivery, quality, meeting needs, market trends, costs, and profits.

No matter how good a deal the other party may be getting from you, if they feel you are getting more than you deserve from them, they will do anything and everything possible to make sure that you don't get what they don't think you deserve—even if you do in fact deserve it. That is simply the way most of us are.

Let's be the Myers as buyers of this house for a moment. We make an offer that is decidedly under what the Brownings have offered their home for. We are sure that they will perceive it as a low-ball offer, so we want to preempt this from happening if we can. Here are some of the things that we can incorporate into our offer:

> We assure the Brownings that we are not telling them what their property is worth, only what it is worth to us. That way we eliminate any chances of offending them on this issue of price.

> Or we could explain to them that we are limited by our budget, and that is all that we can afford to spend. Most of us understand the general concept of budget and staying (at least theoretically) on budget.

> If your offer is really high or low, you can temper it by suggesting there is some flexibility in it. For example, you might say, "We can only afford to pay X for your property at this time, the way the market presently is." "That is all we can pay for the home according to our current plans." "That is the most we can offer, as we see it."

VALUE IS IN THE EYE OF THE BEHOLDER.

"At this time, the way the market conditions are" implies that if the market conditions were to get better, then you might be able to agree to something more favorable to the other party. "According to our current plans" suggests that there could be flexibility in future plans. "As we see it" hints that we might see it differently later.

Leaving the door ajar gives us the possibility of renegotiating at a later time.

An additional problem in making out-of-place high demands or low-ball offers is that they are hard to defend. Generally you want to have a strong rationale for each demand. The rationale is the justification, the reasons why they should give you what you are asking for. If it is an unreasonable, off-the-wall demand that is going to be really hard to justify other than by simply saying, "That is what I want," your demand will not be particularly strong in the other party's eyes.

OUT-OF-PLACE DEMANDS

*Anybody can become angry—that is easy:
But to be angry with the right person, and to the right degree, and at the right time, and for the right purpose, and in the right way—that is not within everybody's power and is not easy.*
   —Aristotle

39

Give concessions that are of high value to the other party and which cost you little

MAKING A CONCESSION can be a golden opportunity to get something greater in return. Strive to make this mutually so, not only for you but for your counterpart. Mutually beneficial relationships take place when the parties have compatible concerns and interests: I want to sell my home, and you want to buy it. I want to have children in our marriage, and you do likewise. I don't want to run this business, and you do. You want to start your real estate investment plan by purchasing a duplex, and I want to sell and be able to travel more in later years.

Note that sometimes the interests are the same—going out together on a date; sometimes they are different—I have a house to sell, and you have money and desire to buy it.

The greater your like-mindedness is to your counterpart, the greater opportunities there are to put win-win transactions together.

How does this relate to making concessions that cost you little and gain them much? It is due to the compatibility of interests: They value something you have more

> **People will make demands of all kinds on you as long as you allow them to.**

HIGH-VALUE CONCESSIONS 153

> **SEARCH OUT COMPATIBLE PARTIES WITH WHOM YOU HAVE SIMILAR INTERESTS AND DO BUSINESS WITH THEM.**

than you value it, and they have something that you value more than they do in exchange.

Examples are numerous: I arrange to give your organization a negotiating session that will vastly improve the ability of your salespeople to make better and more profitable agreements, and you pay me a fee. I give you a library of books that I no longer want, which you want badly. I give you my used car that you badly need and that I don't want around anymore. And on it goes.

It makes sense to search out those parties with whom we have similar interests and do business with them.

Should I let the other party know that what I am giving them in the exchange costs me little and gives them much? Be careful on both sides of this. First, letting them know that it costs you little (which does not mean that you don't value it, but simply that it costs you little for any number of reasons) might diminish, in their eyes, the value of what you have given them. Second, if you attempt to show them how much value this has for them, they might resist such an evaluation and argue that no, it hasn't. At times it may be better to guide them and let them discover it on their own.

Questions to your counterpart can be like these: "Frederick, how does your company plan to use this item you are buying from us?" Or "Frederick, how does this product fit into your overseas business?" You could possibly mention, "The Sorenson group has found that by using this product in their print media advertising, they have received wonderful results. Might that possibly work for you?"

Strive, in making concessions, to give high value to the other party and minimize the cost to yourself. What is it that you have that they want and could benefit by and that they would take in an exchange that costs you little?

Simply asking ourselves or, in some cases, the other party that question directs attention to something that may have been overlooked at first but becomes obvious on second glance.

> *Sow much, reap much; sow little, reap little.*
> —Chinese proverb

Section VI

Power, Tricks & Ploys

40. Beware of a biting dog.
41. Escalating authority.
42. Good Guy/Bad Guy ploy.
43. Power and traps of deadlines.
44. Don't let anyone steal your joy.
45. Know who the enemy is!
46. Power of legitimacy in the written word.

40

BEWARE OF A BITING DOG

I SUSPECT MOST OF US believe that when possible, win-win negotiation is the best way to go. Both parties benefit and gain for having negotiated with each other. Zig Ziglar, a popular and masterful teacher, often remarks, "You can get everything you want in life if you'll just help enough other people get what they want." Certainly a win-win philosophy. The double win, as Denis Waitley refers to it, is admirable, and the Win-Win or No DEAL, which Stephen Covey writes about in *The Seven Habits of Highly Effective People,* is to be coveted and worked toward, most would argue.

It's certainly hard to find fault with such a mind-set, and it's one that is recommended whenever possible. But there will be times when a win-win may not be possible, at least at first sitting. There are times when we all must beware of the "biting dog" before we will be able to get to win-win, if at all.

A sage Japanese Zen master taught his students: "God is everything. God is Love and out of that love he made the universe and you in his likeness. All is love, all is God." Returning home after the teaching, one of the students met a vicious dog. Thinking of the master's teaching of love and remembering that he as a person was made in the image of God, he extended his hand in love and trust to the growling dog.

The dog immediately bit his hand and tore the flesh of other body parts. Bleeding, bewildered, and angered,

BEWARE OF THE MAN WHO CARRIES THE BIGGEST BIBLE.

LESSON 1

NOBODY TOLD THE DOG.

the student quickly returned to his master teacher and related his woeful tale. The master said to the student, "You may have known that you were made in God's image and love, but nobody told the dog."

You may know in negotiation that a win-win is possible, but has anyone told the other party? Beware of the "biting dog" who sees negotiating as win-lose—that is, they are supposed to win and you are supposed to lose. Some define negotiating as beating the other person or winning more or losing less than the other party.

If you enter into negotiation with this type of party, they are the "biting dog." Before attempting to negotiate win-win, you need to change the "biting dog" attitude toward you in the particular negotiation in which you are involved with them. No trusting, sharing unilaterally, or being a nice guy is going to get the biting dog to change on the spot. In fact, more than likely the biting dog will see these kinds of win-win approaches as an open invitation to eat your lunch—or you, to use a figure of speech.

Don't assume they wear the mantle of Mother Teresa. My father used to say, "Beware of the man who carries the biggest Bible." Not all is what it may seem to be. Check it out.

It is very possible and even probable, in this complex, competitive world, that the party does not wish you joy and celebration. Or at least they are not going out of their way to wish that to you. They might well be that "biting dog." Beware! Or at least, be aware.

BEWARE! OR AT LEAST, BE AWARE.

Talk to others who have negotiated with this party. Go slowly at first. Ask them what they want by accomplish negotiating with you. Guard your Best Option Outside Negotiation (BOON) with them. Do your due diligence and don't look to others to do for you what you should be doing for yourself.

Just because the dog is wagging his tail and licking your hand doesn't mean he isn't going to bite you later.

—Anonymous

41

ESCALATING AUTHORITY

IMAGINE FOR A MINUTE that you have just finished negotiating a contract agreement with Harold, assistant purchasing manager, in the conference room of his Bellflower electronics firm. He excuses himself and leaves the room. You think, "I guess Harold has gone down the hall to go to the bathroom or take a smoke."

A few seconds later, in comes Harold's manager, Helen Escalator. You immediately think to yourself, "Gee, that is nice of Harold's boss to come in and congratulate us on completing our negotiation." No, because in just a few seconds you realize that is not why Harold's manager is in the room with you.

"Rob," she says, "I just looked over the agreement you and Harold have reached. I feel so bad, Rob, but Harold had no authority to agree to purchase 1,000 units of electronic components at those prices. At most we could commit to 500, and those 500 units would have to be at least 15 percent reduced from the price in this agreement.

"Also, Rob, I don't know what Harold was thinking of, in fact he probably wasn't, when he said we could give you $25 a unit for the Conlan transistors. That is not possible. And by the way, payment terms must be further extended, as we have cash flow difficulties now and for the foreseeable future."

Before Harold's boss can continue this litany of changing the just-signed agreement, you respond, "Thank you

WILLINGNESS TO SAY "NO DEAL" GIVES YOU POWER IN THE NEGOTIATING ARENA.

for sharing that information with me, Helen. You know, I, too, was wondering about Harold's heredity background and his IQ. Am I glad that you as his boss are here! Now we can start right over and renegotiate the whole contract from scratch." Or, "Thank you, Helen, for letting me know about Harold's deficiencies. I, too, was concerned about the validity of the agreement, so null and void the contract and call it a day."

Recall that the one thing that gives you real power in the negotiating arena is your willingness to walk—your willingness to say, "No deal, I am out of here and on my way to my Best Option Outside Negotiation" (that is, your BOON).

What happened here was a switch not just of negotiators but a basic abrogation of the ostensibly completed negotiation and signed agreement. A higher and supposedly more intimidating, more powerful, more authentic decisionmaker has come in and picked up the negotiation and begun making serious changes in the agreements. And all the changes the escalator makes are not in your favor. In fact, in every case they work against you. No one needs to bring to your attention that if Helen gets away with this, it will be very much at your expense.

Tell the escalator authority that you are glad they are here so you can begin the negotiation all over again with someone who really has the authority to make the agreements and close the deal. In that way, you are not challenging this escalated situation.

➤ You might call in your own escalator, possibly your boss.

➤ Go down the hall and disappear as Harold did.

➤ Walk out of the office with the original agreement intact and act as if that is the true and only agreement.

WATCH OUT FOR A HIGHER AUTHORITY-LEVEL SWITCH— IT'S A PLOY.

View escalating authority as a ploy well thought out and rehearsed beforehand. Its aim is to draw you into a false sense of security—of believing you have a deal. Then, the escalated higher authority is pulling on you, demanding more concessions and taking back some agreements already made.

Let us never negotiate out of fear.
But let us never fear to negotiate.
—John F. Kennedy

42

Good Guy/ Bad Guy ploy

WHAT DO YOU THINK of when someone says they did a Good Guy/Bad Guy ploy? Perhaps a police officer interrogating a suspect at the police station: The room is dark except for a bright light beamed onto the suspect's face. There, berating him, intimidating him, ripping him up one side and down the other (figuratively if not literally), is the sergeant, the Bad Guy.

He is interrogating the suspect, accusing him, ridiculing him, drilling him about the crime he has committed, working to get a confession.

Then, guess who comes on the scene: the Good Cop. He turns on the light, goes over to Harold the bad cop, and says, "Sergeant Harold, get out of here. You can't treat James that way."

Ostensibly, from the suspect's viewpoint, he makes Harold, the bad cop, leave. Now Frank, the good cop, goes up to suspect James and says, "James, look here, I want to help you. I know you have had some bad luck in life. I can appreciate that. But listen, James, for me to help, you are going to have to tell me why you killed her and where you hid the body. Now, James, I know you didn't mean to do it. I know that for you it was an accident. But you have to tell me everything. If you don't, well, James, I will have to leave and Frank will take over again. You don't want that, do you?"

Well, there you have the scene: Harold the bad cop intimidating, and Frank the good cop there to help

DON'T BE DECEIVED: TAKE THEIR GOOD GUY/ BAD GUY PLOY AND USE IT AGAINST THEM.

The Good Guy is really a Bad Guy, in disguise.

James. Of course, in reality they are both bad cops in the sense that they are there to extract a confession out of James. Just different means, same end.

Frank the good cop is working to gain the confidence of James and convince James that the last thing James really wants is to have to deal with terrible, bad cop Harold.

Now, most of us don't get interrogated by the police, at least not very often. But we do make a purchase every few years that almost assures us we will be on the receiving end of the Good Guy/Bad Guy ploy. Right. When you buy a car, who is the good guy? Who is the person who is going to get you the best deal this automobile agency has ever given anyone? Of course, the salesperson. And who is the bad guy, the person the salesperson is going to have to go to battle against to get you the best deal ever? The sales manager.

You know the ploy. Walk into the showroom. The salesperson, friendly and helpful, asks you what you want in a car, shows you your car, gives you the keys to take it for a run. Then you sit down in the closing room, and what happens? He strikes a good deal with you, but he has to check it out with his manager. He comes back very apologetic. He can't do the deal, but if you could see your way clear ... and on the story goes.

In business negotiations, you may have the occasion to see two members of your counterpart team. One is the nicest person you have ever dealt with. Maybe you would even like your son or daughter to marry that kind of person. The other seems to be the devil incarnate. Boisterous, intimidating, the kind who stonewalls you and continually hammers you for more and strives to give you less. Simply not a pleasant person at all to work with.

It's the same thing. Both are really bad, but each is playing a role, hoping to take advantage of you.

Countermeasures are many, all the way from sitting back to see how well they do the Good Guy/Bad Guy routine to bringing your own Good Guy/Bad Guy in or refusing to negotiate with them as long as they use that ploy.

Don't be deceived. Take their ploy and use it against them. You could feed wrong and detrimental information to the so-called Good Guy, in confidence, of course, knowing that the Bad Guy will have this information in a New York minute.

There may be times when you will want to use this technique. Then we would not call it a ploy; we would call it a negotiating strategy. For instance, parents might play Good Guy/Bad Guy. For example, you say to your thirteen-year-old son, "Look, if we can't reach agreement on when you are going to clean up your bedroom and when you are going to look at TV and do your homework, then when your mom comes home—you know, the Wicked Witch of the West—when she comes flying in here on a broomstick and her hair is blowing in the wind, and the wind isn't blowing, you know you'll be in deep trouble. It will be out of Dad's hands then." Dad is playing the Good Guy and casting Mom in the role of Bad Guy. Does it work? Sure it can.

Whoopi Goldberg made a movie, *The Associate,* in which she created a fictitious male partner, Robert Cutty. Now she could deal with the male investors and defer to Robert Cutty, so that she could gain the respect so deserved from clients in the investment arena.

The Good Guy/Bad Guy was employed by potential clients when they said to Whoopi, "Gee, it looks good to me, and if it were up to me, I would go for it, but you know my partner, Harold. Harold won't go for it." There probably is no Harold. It is a way of making Harold look bad so you get to look good.

WHEN YOU USE GOOD GUY/BAD GUY, LET'S CALL IT A TECHNIQUE AND NOT A PLOY.

Whoopi, in return, would use her fictitious Robert Cutty—who no one, obviously, was able to meet—as the tough guy. He was the person who always made the important decisions and had the power to make the deals.

So when you see Good Guy/Bad Guy, don't fall for it. Recognize it for what it is: an effort to manipulate you in the manipulator's best perceived interests.

> *The first and great commandment is: Don't let them scare you.*
> —Elmer Davis

43

POWER AND TRAPS OF DEADLINES

NEVER LET TIME be used against you, whether it be setting a deadline by the other party, running out of time, missing your deadline, or missing the other party's deadline.

Specifically, in this lesson we look at the use of setting time limits and deadlines in negotiating.

Have you noticed how deadlines can propel things to get done? Take April 15, when for most of us the IRS has decreed that our taxes are due. It is amazing how many of us wait until the last minute to get our taxes in. Some wait literally until the last minute.

When some of my children were young, on April 15 we played a game. If they had done their schoolwork and taken a nap in the late afternoon, that evening of April 15 we would have a late dinner, then all go down to the main Post Office in Los Angeles and watch the scene unfold on the steps of the Post Office. For several hours before midnight, cars and people would be lined up as people dropped off their returns. Extra Postal Service personnel would stand on the street corners and in the street dividers, taking mail as the cars drove by.

Just before midnight—the tax witching hour—we could see people climbing the steps to the Post Office with pen in one hand and their short form in the other hand, filling out their returns.

In one case we saw several people pounding on the door of the Post Office after the hour of midnight had

LEVERAGE TIME AND DEADLINES TO YOUR ADVANTAGE.

POWER AND TRAPS OF DEADLINES 167

CLARIFY HOW TIME IS PERCEIVED AND WHAT IT MEANS IN THE NEGOTIATION.

struck, demanding that the Postal Service take their now-late returns and back-postmark them to before midnight.

Deadlines can be powerful in getting a specific task done or terminated. In negotiating as in life—use that fact to your advantage. Putting a target date on a proposed agreement can facilitate gaining an agreement and free up time for other important things.

Negotiations have a way of getting bogged down. Deadlines, when properly used, can expedite the negotiation. Like anything in negotiation, as in life, using deadlines can backfire. It can cause such a tense atmosphere that either or both parties can abort the negotiating process under the stress and pressure of a deadline.

It is important that we know how to use deadlines. When to use them and when to refuse them. Make time work for you and not against you. Don't let time be a jailer; let it be a liberator.

When you want someone to get back to you on a certain issue, state, "Marilyn, when could you get back to me with your decision?" Or "When can I expect you to get back to me on this matter?" Or "I will need to have your response by Wednesday no later than 3:00 P.M. so that I can meet my deadlines."

Whether or not you give a reason for the deadline, or the full reason, of course depends on the situation. One of the advantages of giving a reason is that the other party can understand why it is important for them to meet this deadline. You might also spell out in appropriate terms the implications or results if they do or don't meet the deadline and help them to identify with why the deadline is necessary.

Conversely, giving the reason for the deadline—the real or not-so-real one—might cause the other party to argue with you. They might say, "You really don't need to get that information to your group that early." Or "Based on our experience, you don't need to have this information until two weeks from now."

So, if you think they will attempt to use your reason against you, don't give it to them unless absolutely forced to. When that happens, work to be in as much control of the reason as you can. "Does that work for you? Okay, great, I will make note in my time planner that you will let me know no later than 3:00 P.M., Wednesday the 15th. Is that agreeable to you? Good."

Do not accept vague timelines like "Rob, we will get it to you as soon as we can" or "We will call you as soon as we know." When you hear that and even when it is true, you can strive to get further clarification and agreements, such as: "Fine, Richard, when do you anticipate that might be? Oh, you don't know. Can we then agree that you will call me next Friday at 11:00 A.M. with an update, even if that update is simply to say you know nothing further? I have a great need to be kept informed and to know that we are still working on this together. Is that agreeable to you, Richard?" "Great, then I will put on my daily planner to look forward to a call from you at 11:00 A.M. Now if that gets changed, would you please let me know? Great. Good working with you, and we will be talking, if not before, then on Friday at 11:00 A.M."

This is important to you. Tell me, what does "I will get back to you as soon as I know something" mean to you? That could be tomorrow, or next week, or a month, or a year, or never, couldn't it? They—your counterpart—will get back when they think it is to their advantage to get back to you and not necessarily when they think it is to your advantage. As a matter of fact, getting back to you, may in part be based on when they think it works worst for you and best for them, irrespective of when they have the information in question.

DEADLINES CAN FACILITATE GETTING AGREEMENTS SIGNED.

When it is to your advantage, work to get a more definite time frame.

Now, I suppose the other side of this deadline thing is that, when it is not to your advantage to have a deadline set, then work to avoid discussing and/or agreeing with one.

I get involved in negotiating 1031 tax-deferred real estate exchanges on a regular basis. Time and timing can be very critical, as the IRS guidelines are very specific and unbending in the time allowed for the properties to be transferred in a real estate tax-deferred exchange.

In one exchange my group was running against a deadline—a deadline that if not met would completely trigger a taxable event on properties that would be not just onerous, but also devastating to the estate-building process.

Although we wanted the other party to know we faced a deadline they had to meet or we would go with an alternative property, we didn't want that other party to think they had our backs to the wall. Deadlines were an important part of getting all agreements signed and closing the negotiation before a certain time. Severe penalties were in place for the selling party, if they did not meet their time obligations to us in this 1031 tax-deferred exchange. We also did not fully disclose to them what our Best Option Outside Negotiation (BOON) was, as it frankly wasn't very good. Also, they might well have used it against us by driving a harder bargain, holding up the sale, pushing us to the time limit so we would be forced to make concessions under duress to meet our tax deadlines. Besides, it wasn't any of their business.

In our offer, we had put down that this offer to them to buy their property could be preempted by another nonrelated offer we had out, so time was of the essence.

Since that particular 1031 tax-deferred real estate exchange, I have worked assiduously to avoid facing such deadlines in other exchanges.

Use deadlines to your advantage and reap the rewards. At a minimum, do not let others use deadlines against you to your disadvantage.

> *Nine-tenths of wisdom consists in being wise in time.*
> —Theodore Roosevelt

44

Don't let anyone steal your joy

"Don't let anyone steal your joy" rings loud, clear, true, and important in the competitive, complex, changing world we live in as we move into the twenty-first century.

Negotiating can be stressful, discouraging, and even frightening. Accusations are made, promises broken, gambits and ploys and tricks played out at the negotiating table.

Most of us had to reach agreements with people who were not particularly easy to work with, who were even disagreeable and maybe even not out to wish us joy and celebration. There are people in this world who will attempt to manipulate you and intimidate you. They will almost certainly do so if you encourage them by your behavior and your attitude of giving them the okay.

However difficult, acrimonious, demanding, or unfair a negotiation might be from your point of view, guard closely your feelings and sense of self-worth and self-esteem.

There are those with whom we come into contact who will do us harm. They will cheat and lie to us if it furthers their own self-proclaimed ends. Some difficult or unkind people seem to take a certain perverse sense of joy and accomplishment when they can scare you. The first law and commandment at this juncture is "Don't let them scare you, and don't let them steal your joy."

I was in a particularly difficult business time with my direct-mail marketing firms. Our business had expanded beyond all my comprehension. One of our management development programs had been so universally accepted, both nationally and internationally, that it had driven revenues as well as expenses beyond our ability to manage it well. I was having particular difficulty with some of my firm's top management staff, staff that I had personally hired but who saw things differently. We didn't share the same hopes and dreams for the company. As the days of stress continued and constant friction between myself and my management team grew, I found I enjoyed less and less what I had committed my professional life to.

Members of the board of directors were acutely aware of the impact this stress and loss of vision were having on me and the friction that was evident between me and my top management team. It was affecting everything that we were trying to do as an organization. The negative strain and stress of working with my employees took its toll on my health.

At the conclusion of one of the board meetings, a key trusted board member pulled me aside and said, "Rob, don't let anyone steal your joy." I walked away from that meeting and went outside to be by myself. "Don't let anyone steal your joy" rang in my head. It hit me. That was it. That was what I had allowed to happen in the constant negotiation and renegotiation I was having, not only with my top management team but also with some of the long-term employees. I had allowed them to steal my joy. Whose fault was that? Whose problem was that to solve? Not theirs, but mine.

I immediately affirmed, "I do not let anyone steal my joy. My joy is mine and only mine to behold. I acknowledge that my joy is totally under my control. I can choose to let others steal it from me, but that is my choice, not theirs.

"I can also take back that choice of allowing others to steal my joy. I acknowledge that no one can steal my joy without my permission. Permission refused."

WHEN OTHERS ARE STEALING YOUR JOY, LET THEM KNOW.

STEALING YOUR JOY

173

I walked back into my office building, up to my office, and began discussions with my top management team that were more productive for all concerned. Peace of mind and a sense of well-being and being in control of my own destiny were reaffirmed.

Don't let anyone steal your joy. Like so many things in this book and in greater life, it's much easier said than done.

How do I protect my joy? Know what brings me joy and know what takes joy away. As we all are different, what might take away my joy might not affect yours at all. Knowing ourselves and letting others know what we want and do not want in any relationship, during or out of formal negotiations, is paramount. Equally important is knowing what creates a sense of satisfaction, accomplishment, and joy. Work to increase those factors. For example, if what brings you joy is to have others include you in the decision-making process, let them know that and be prepared to add to the decision-making process. If in negotiating you are affected by certain remarks or kinds of stories, let the other party know that. Be prepared to deal with such to protect your joy.

When others are stealing your joy, let them know. It is possible they don't realize that what they are doing is stealing your joy. Joy is something personal. What brings me delight, happiness, serenity, and a sense of satisfaction might be quite different in a negotiation from what brings those feelings to someone else. So let them know. The other parties are not mind readers. They may simply not recognize that when they are not prepared, or when they don't say thank you, or when they constantly talk about some minor issue that robs you of joy. Even when it looks as if they are intentionally "rattling your cage," "raining on your parade," or however you wish to describe it, they may not know. Let them know in ways that encourage them to stop doing what they are doing to impinge on your joy.

In one particular negotiation, Party B was making veiled threats and putting forth innuendoes about the honesty and integrity of Party A. Party A took that personally and became extremely upset. Yet, failing to deal with this attack led to further deterioration not only of Party A but of the results of the negotiation—results that were far too advantageous to Party B and unwarranted by any fair, objective standard. These results were simply or at least in great part due to the fact that Party A had allowed Party B to intimidate them, take advantage of them, and steal their joy.

Much or all of this could have been avoided if, during the negotiation, Party A had confronted Party B and called them on this. "Should I take what you just said as a personal insult?" "Should I take what you just said as a threat?" "How would you like me to interpret what you are saying?" "Should I take it as meaning that I cannot trust you to live up to your agreements?" "What evidence do you have that would support your demands?"

"Harold, I want to change the direction of this discussion. I feel that what you have said and are proposing is an effort to manipulate me, to intimidate me, and to attack my personal integrity. Is that a correct assessment?"

See yourself as in total control of your own destiny. Visualize the peace of mind you have when you take care of yourself and refuse to allow others to take away your joy and celebration both in and out of the negotiating arena.

Give us clear vision that we may know where to stand and what to stand for because unless we stand for something, we shall fall for anything.
—Peter Marshall

45

KNOW WHO THE ENEMY IS!

HAROLD WAS REPRESENTING a group of real estate investors who had made an offer to buy sixteen condominiums that had recently been foreclosed on by the bank that had made the original loans. These real estate–owned properties were in need of substantial repair; they were empty, the market was depressed, and investors were wary of the future economic value of the units.

The bank officers saw the offer as a rip-off, as an attempt to take advantage of the bank and the fact that the bank had had to take back the properties and the market was bad and its future clouded at best. The bank's counteroffer to Harold's group was couched in adversarial, harsh, and unreasonable terms: For example, a default on any one of the sixteen condominium loans would constitute a default on the other fifteen loans, a demand for several thousand dollars to be put down as security on each of the sixteen condominiums, with the provision that a default on one constituted a default on all sixteen, and the security deposit on all of them would be owed. And on it went. Clearly, the bank saw the buying party and the investors as THE ENEMY!

How much chance do you think there was for the two parties—Harold's investors and the bank—to reach a win-win agreement as long as one saw the other as the enemy? Little or none. So the investment group had the

IS IT POSSIBLE THAT YOU MIGHT BE YOUR OWN WORST ENEMY?

challenge—which they met—of demonstrating to the bank that they, the investors, were not the enemy but rather, in a sense, the saviors. The real enemies were the bad economic conditions, the fact that the bank had made loans too high a few years before and not qualified its borrowers as strictly as it might have, and the fact that the properties were left in poor repair, as the owners foreclosed on were not happy about losing their properties.

Most of us have seen scenes of bullfights in Spain and Mexico. The toreador stands there bravely, waving a red cape, egging the unsuspecting bull on to battle and ultimate death (for the bull, that is, and in rare cases also for the matador).

Who does the bull think the enemy is? The red cape, not the matador. The bull charges the red cape as if his life depended on it. He charges, snarls, shifts his hooves in the arena dirt, all the time thinking that the red cape is his enemy, but of course it is not. The red cape has never killed a bull in the history of bullfighting. The matador, of course, has, using the cape as a decoy to anger and rile the bull.

When negotiating, keep in mind who the enemy, if any, is. You may be attacking the wrong thing. If there is an enemy—be it someone who wishes you illl, economic conditions that must be overcome, or a negotiating member of the opposite party out to make sure that no one wins in the negotiation—the enemy must be identified and dealt with effectively before any win-win will be achieved.

Is it possible that you are the enemy—your own worst enemy—in a given negotiation? There is a wonderful four-panel cartoon that first shows a person with arms held up to the heavens, saying, "Destroy my enemies, oh God"; in the second panel, "God, grant my only request. Destroy my worst enemy"; in panel three, ZAP—a bolt of lightning comes down from heaven; and

IN THE BULLFIGHT ARENA, THE BULL DOES NOT KNOW WHO HIS REAL ENEMY IS.

KNOW WHO THE ENEMY IS

in the fourth panel there is a pile of ashes remaining where the person had stood, and the frame says, "Let me rephrase that."

Sometimes we are, in fact, our own worst enemies in negotiating: We assume, at times incorrectly, that the other party will not give us what we want or that we are weaker or stronger than we really are; we take things personally and walk out when we could have put a good deal together, and on the list goes.

In our example, the real estate agreement was finalized, but not until the buying party was able to show clearly to the bank officers that they, the buying party, were not the enemy. The buyers correctly pointed out in ways the bank could see and agree to that the real enemy had been an extraordinarily harsh economic down market and that the loans more than likely had been too generous at the time they were made.

The buyers were also able to show the bank officials that it was in the bank's best interest to get these properties out of its portfolio, as the bank was not in the business of owning and managing foreclosed real estate.

When you are seen as the enemy in a negotiation and you are not, it is generally not good for any of the parties involved to allow that misconception to persist. You are challenged to show clearly and convincingly that you are not the enemy, and if there is an enemy, to show who or what that is.

Never confuse your banker with Mother Teresa.
—Anonymous

46

POWER OF LEGITIMACY IN THE WRITTEN WORD

AS A YOUNG MAN, I purchased my first real estate investment property, a small, older duplex. When the sale was closed, the tenants on both sides immediately moved out, and I couldn't get the same rent they were paying. Later I found out they were relatives of the previous owner. Another real estate lesson learned: Check out the rents and who the renters are before purchasing a property.

In any event, I advertised my unit for rent in the local newspaper. When a prospective tenant came over, I would explain that four-legged animals such as dogs and cats were not allowed, as I didn't want them to mess up my newly acquired property. "What do you want us to do, kid, shoot our dog?" I would hear them say. So I would scratch off that item on my handwritten agreement. Then I said, "You realize, of course, there is a ninety-day, nonrefundable deposit required; that is, if you don't stay at least ninety days, you don't get your deposit back." "You young whippersnapper, what are you trying to do—rip us off?" So that item would be crossed off my handwritten agreement.

I couldn't get anyone to sign the agreement. One day a friend of mine said, "Rob, why don't you go to the Board of Realtors here in Santa Barbara and ask them for help?" "What is a Board of Realtors?" I asked. "They are

TO SOME, IF IT IS IN WRITING, IT MUST BE TRUE.

Preprinted forms can work miracles.

real estate brokers and salespeople who belong to the board." So I called them and explained my situation. They said they couldn't help me because I was not a member; however, they said I could simply go down to Banks' Stationery store on State Street and get myself some preprinted rental forms. Then, when a prospective renter came by, I could simply fill in the blank spaces.

So I got the forms, and when the next prospective tenant came by, I simply filled in the blank spaces on the preprinted form. "And, of course, you realize, sir, there are no four-legged animals like dogs and cats allowed."

"What do you mean, no dogs or cats; what the heck do you want us to do with our dog, shoot him?" And I would respond, "No, sir, it is okay," and I would shove the preprinted contract in front of them and dutifully point out the section that stated no cats and dogs allowed on the premises. And they would say, "Oh, it states that right here, Mary. Okay." And then I would say, "And of course you understand that there is a ninety-day, nonrefundable security deposit clause; that is, if you move before ninety days are up, you don't get your deposit back." "You young whippersnapper," they would say, "what are you trying to do, rip us off?" "No, sir, you see in this clause on page two, section twelve, it clearly states your deposit is not refundable if you leave before ninety days." "Oh, I guess it is okay then," they would concede.

The legitimacy of the written word can be awesome. It seems to some that if it is in writing, it must be true.

In negotiated contracts, whoever draws up the contract almost inevitably is the one who is advantaged by the wording. If you don't draw up the contract, be sure that you read the one given you extra carefully. Know beforehand that it will be biased in favor of the party who drew up the contact.

When your negotiation is concluded, write a memorandum of agreement that outlines the key points of the agreements. If you err, you will generally err in your favor. If you leave something out, it is generally something that was not particularly good for you. If you included something that was not really agreed to during the actual negotiations, it will most likely work in your favor. I'm not suggesting that you purposely lie or leave things out or add things, but the advantage and favor, favorable omission, and commission of error generally go to the agreement writer.

Use the power of legitimacy, then, to your advantage. You be the one to write out the contract, memorandum of agreement, letter of intent, or whatever it might be. When you do that, it becomes incumbent on the other party to either contradict, question, or agree to what you have put down.

The converse of this is to watch very carefully the written agreements, notes, and memorandums of agreement that are sent to you. The time to take exception to any omission or commission of error is immediately upon receiving a document. You can work to leverage the receipt of such a written notification by becoming upset that something was included and renegotiate some other items out that you didn't want in the first place.

LET THE WRITTEN WORD DO YOUR SPEAKING FOR YOU.

> *It is not what you don't know what gets you into trouble: It's what you know for sure that ain't so.*
> —Mark Twain

About the Author

Robert D. Rutherford, Ph.D., is an accomplished teacher, businessman, and author who has consulted with and trained tens of thousands of professionals. A former faculty member of the University of California at Los Angeles and the California Institute of Technology, he has also served as Director of Executive Education at the Graduate School of Management, UCLA. Dr. Rutherford has been a real estate executive, television talk-show host, and was president of one of the nation's largest management seminar firms for the public.

His work has been covered in such publications as *Business Week* and *The Wall Street Journal*, and has been syndicated throughout the United States and translated into several foreign languages.

As president of Rutherford Group International, Dr. Rutherford conducts training seminars on negotiations and management development for executives and managers in a variety of small and large organizations nationwide. Among the clients he has worked with are California Institute of Technology, Owens Corning, IBM, Lucent Technologies, ARCO, George Washington University, the U.S Navy, National Renewable Energy Laboratories, Warner-Lambert, Toyota, Prudential HealthCare, and many others.

His other books include *Just in Time: Immediate Help for the Time Pressured; Twenty-Five Most Common Mistakes Made in Negotiating ... and What You Can Do About Them;* and *The Price Myth: How to Sell at Top Prices, Negotiate Like the Pros, and Leave the Competition Behind.*

FOR KEYNOTES, TALKS, SEMINARS & PRODUCTS

For more information on Dr. Rutherford's keynote addresses, talks, seminars, and products, simply contact him through his firm: Rutherford Group International (RGI) of Boulder, Colorado. RGI offers both publicly and privately held negotiating, sales, and management training designed to increase personal and organizational effectiveness.

Contact Rob Rutherford at

RGI
1195 Fairfield Drive • Suite 100
Boulder, Colorado 80303
TEL: 303.494.9444
FAX: 303.494.9408
E-MAIL: Roobd@aol.com
www.Rob-Rutherford.com